From the End of the World to the Ends of the Earth

© 2004 Stefan Höschele

All rights reserved. No part of this publication may be reproduced, stored in a retrieval system, or transmitted in any form or by any means, electronic, mechanical, photocopying, recording or otherwise, without prior permission from the publishers.

Published by
Kachere Series,
P.O. Box 1037, Zomba, Malawi
ISBN-10: 99908-76-11-8
ISBN-13: 978-99908-76-11-6

Layout: Gladys Phiri
Cover Design: Mercy Chilunga
Graphic Design: Patrick Lichakala

Printed by Lightning Source

From the End of the World to the Ends of the Earth

The Development of Seventh-Day Adventist Missiology

Stefan Höschele

Kachere Studies no. 6

Kachere Series,
P.O. Box 1037, Zomba, Malawi
kachere@globemw.net
www.sdnp.org.mw/kachereseries/

This book is part of the Kachere Series, a range of books on religion, culture and society in Malawi. Other Kachere books are:

Joseph Booth, *Africa for the African* (1897), ed. Laura Perry, reprint

Harry Langworthy, *"Africa for the African". The Life of Joseph Booth*

Yonah Matemba, *The History of Matandani Seventh-day Adventist Mission*

J.C. Chakanza, *Voices of Preachers in Protest. The Ministry of Two Malawian Prophets: Elliot Kamwana and Wilfred Gudu*

Klaus Fiedler, *Christianity and African Culture: Conservative German Protestant Missionaries in Tanzania, 1900-1940*

Stephen Kauta Msiska, *Golden Buttons: Christianity and Traditional Religion among the Tumbuka*

George Shepperson and Thomas Price, *Independent African. John Chilembwe and the Nyasaland Rising of 1915*

Hilary Mijoga, *Separate but Same Gospel. Preaching in African Instituted Churches in Southern Malawi*

Henry Church, *Theological Education that Makes a Difference. Church Growth in the Free Methodist Church in Malawi and Zimbabwe*

The Kachere Series is the publications arm of the Department of Theology and Religious Studies of the University of Malawi.

Series Editors: J.C. Chakanza, Fulata L. Moyo, F.L. Chingota, Klaus Fiedler, P.A. Kalilombe, Martin Ott, Shareef Mahomed

Series Editors' Preface

The Kachere Series started in 1995 as an initiative of the Department of Theology and Religious Studies at the University of Malawi. Its aim was—and still is—to promote the emergence of a body of literature which will enable students and others to engage critically with religion in Malawi, its social impact and the theological questions which it raises; however, in recent years its remit has been widened to encompass books on culture and society as well. An important starting point lies with the publication of essays and theses that until now have been inaccessible to all but the most dedicated specialist. It is also hoped that the development of theological and cultural scholarship in Malawi will stimulate the writing of many new books.

General works with popular appeal can be published as *Kachere Books*. Documents and essays, which are of value as sources for the study of religion in Malawi, can be published as *Kachere Texts*. Full-length treatises, the fruit of sound primary research which meet rigorous academic standards, are published as *Kachere Monographs*, and books with a more general appeal, but not necessarily dealing with Malawi, can be published as *Kachere Studies*.

The editors intend the Series to contribute substantially to the growth of a body of knowledge in the area of theology and religious studies in Malawi. As important resources for study related to this field, we are confident that they will come to be prized not only within Malawi but also in every academic centre concerned with religion and society in Africa.

Kachere Series Editors
Zomba, Advent 2003

Contents

SERIES EDITORS' PREFACE 5

PREFACE 8

INTRODUCTION 9

CHAPTER 1 13
The Historical Development of Adventist Mission and Underlying Theological Emphases 13

CHAPTER 2 29
Systematic Aspects 29

CHAPTER 3 41
Some Current Issues and Recent Developments 41

CHAPTER 4 62
Final Remarks: The Future of Seventh-Day Adventist Missiology 62

APPENDIX I: MISSION STATEMENT OF THE SEVENTH-DAY ADVENTIST CHURCH 66

APPENDIX II: "THE REMNANT AND ITS MISSION" 67

ANNOTATED BIBLIOGRAPHY 68
Publications by Adventists Referred to 68
Magazines 74
Articles and Unpublished Materials 75
Further Reference Materials 79
Evangelism and Church Growth 79

Abbreviations

AEA	Archiv für Europäische Adventgeschichte, Friedensau
ANN	*Adventist News Network*
AR	*Adventist Review*, 1978-
AU	Andrews University, Berrien Springs
AUP	Andrews University Press, Berrien Springs
AV	Advent-Verlag, Hamburg
GC	General Conference
JATA	*Journal of Adventist Thought in Africa*, 1996-
NIV	*The Bible*, New International Version
PPPA	Pacific Press Publishing, Mountain View
RH	*[Second] [Advent] Review and [Sabbath] Herald*, 1850-1977
RHPA	Review and Herald Publishing Association, Washington D.C./Hagerstown
SDA	Seventh-day Adventist(s)
SDAE	*Seventh-day Adventist Encyclopedia*, RHPA, 1976
SPA	Southern Publishing Association, Nashville
WCC	World Council of Churches

Preface

Although this book was originally intended to be a mere academic exercise, it grew to a size bigger than this intention suggested. One reason for this is that it had been my wish to write on Adventist Missiology even before. The second, and more weighty one, is that Dr Klaus Fiedler, my *Doktorvater*, and his colleagues, the *Kachere* Series editors, encouraged me to have it published. I have appreciated their gentle pushes very much.

What made me particularly happy are the circumstances under which this study grew. It was during my stay in Africa where I worked as a lecturer of theology at Tanzania Adventist College, continuing the Adventist missionary tradition that began one hundred years ago in this country, and while doing doctoral studies of the University of Malawi. There could not have been any more inspiring setting to write on the Missiology of a church that has a higher percentage of adherents in much of Eastern and Central Africa than in most Western countries.

The bibliography has been annotated in the books and magazines sections so that the reader may more easily understand the value of the various references. I wish to thank my friend Pastor Cepha Ang'ira as well as Dr. Erich Baumgartner and Dr Russell Staples, both of Andrews University, for their willingness to comment on and critique the content.

I dedicate this little book to Alina, my wife and foremost partner in mission.

Introduction

The Seventh-day Adventist Church which recently passed the 12 million member mark is a movement that owes much of its identity to a unique Missiology. This short study tries to contribute in a humble way to an understanding of the most important aspects and issues of this Missiology as reflected in Seventh-day Adventist history as well as the present situation of this denomination.

The Advent movement, in spite of its sometimes uniformizing tendencies, has always been diverse, and the more it spread, the larger became the differences in missiological thinking and evangelistic approaches. However, one can find, at least in history, ideas and practices agreed upon by many leading scholars, missionaries, and administrators of the church, in part changing throughout time, but partly constant. Thus, this study has tried to use mainly sources that are to some degree representative without letting marginal developments go unnoticed.

Especially from the beginning of the 20th century, there has been a flood of Seventh-day Adventist books about missionary experiences as well as biographies of missionaries and similar popular materials that did not systematize Adventist Missiology.[1] More recently, especially during the last 30 years, a good number of works that develop SDA missiological thought have appeared.[2] It is, however, not only in

---

[1] E.g.: George F. Enoch, *The Advent Message in the Sunny Caribbean*, Port of Spain, Trinidad: Watchman, 1907; Ludwig R. Conradi et al., *Freud und Leid der Missionare des S.T.A. Missionsgebietes am Viktoriasee*, Hamburg: Internationale Traktatgesellschaft, 1919; William H. Anderson, *On the Trail of Livingstone*, PPPA, 1919; Luise Drangmeister, *Als Lehrerin im afrikanischen Busch*, AV, 1938 [Tanzania]; James Cormack, *Isles of Solomon*, RHPA, 1944; Valdemar E. Toppenberg, *Africa Has My Heart*, PPPA, 1958; T.S. Wangerin, *God Sent Me to Korea*, RHPA, 1968; Robert H. Pierson, [GC President 1966-1978], *Angels over Elisabethville*, PPPA, 1975; Louise van Dyke, *Desert Diary*, RHPA, 1981 [medical work amongst Muslims].

[2] Especially: Bruce L. Bauer, "Congregational and Mission Structures and how the Seventh-Day Adventist Church has Related to Them", DMiss, Pasadena: Fuller Theological Seminary, 1982; Erich W. Baumgartner (ed.), *Re-Visioning Adventist*

this recent past that mission issues have been debated on theologically. Ellen G. White (1827-1915), a major pioneer of the church who called herself "the Lord's messenger"[3] and who is considered to be a prophet by the Seventh-day Adventist Church, has made many statements about the theological basis of mission, mission strategy, and various issues involved in the task and expansion of the Church from the very beginning of the Church's existence. Apart from SDA periodicals, it is mainly due to her rich literary work that we can today establish basic theological tenets that are essential in Seventh-day Adventist Missiology.[4] Apart from her, from the time when the

---

Mission in Europe, AUP 1998; P. Gerard Damsteegt, *Foundations of the Seventh-Day Adventist Message and Mission*, Grand Rapids: Eerdmans, 1977; Hugh I. Dunton, Baldur Ed. Pfeiffer and Borge Schantz (eds.), *Adventist Missions Facing the 21st Century: a Reader*, Frankfurt: Lang, 1990; Jon Dybdahl, *Missions: a Two-Way Street*, PPPA, 1986; Jon Dybdahl (ed.), *Adventist Mission in the 21st Century: The Joys and Challenges of Presenting Jesus to a Diverse World*, RHPA, 1999; Robert E. Firth (ed.), *Servants for Christ: the Adventist Church Facing the Eighties*, AUP, 1980; *Handbuch für Gemeindeaufbau*, 3 vols., Darmstadt, Friedensau: Zentralstelle für Evangelisation und Gemeindeaufbau, 1993; Richard Lehmann, Jack Mahon and Borge Schantz (eds.), *Cast the Net on the Right Side...: Seventh-Day Adventists Face the "Isms" - Crucial Issues for Witnessing to Western People*, Bracknell: European Institute of World Mission, 1993; Gottfried Oosterwal, *Mission: Possible*, SPA, 1972; Humberto Rasi and Fritz Guy (eds.), *Meeting the Secular Mind: Some Adventist Perspectives*, Selected Working Papers of the Committee on Secularism of the General Conference of SDA 1981-1985, AUP, 1985; Borge F. Schantz, "The Development of Seventh-Day Adventist Missionary Thought: Contemporary Appraisal", PhD, Pasadena: Fuller Theological Seminary, 1983. The last title is a 2-volume, 973-page work that mainly studies the historical development of SDA mission theory and Ellen G. White's contribution toward it.

[3] Ellen G. White, *Selected Messages*, Vol. 1, RHPA, 1958, p. 32.

[4] Mentioned should be the following of her works that deal directly with mission and evangelism: *Gospel Workers: Instruction for all who are "Laborers together with God"*, Rev. and enlarged ed., RHPA, 1948 (1st ed. 1892; 2nd ed. 1915); *Evangelism*, RHPA, 1946 [Compilation of different materials written by Ellen G. White]; and *The Southern Work*, RHPA, 1966 [Reprinted from articles and letters of 1891-1899]; see also books like *Welfare Ministry*, RHPA, 1952; *The Ministry of Healing*, RHPA, 1905; *Manual for Canvassers*, RHPA, 1902; and *Christian Service*, RHPA, 1925. Even more fundamental theologically for SDA mission are two of Ellen White's most famous books, *The Desire of Ages*, RHPA, 1898; and *The Great Controversy between Christ and Satan*, PPPA, 1884.

Adventist missionary endeavour started to grow more significant around the turn of the century, there have been also some individuals who engaged in various aspects of research and writing in the fields of - not SDA-specific - mission apologetics,[5] anthropology/ethnology and linguistics,[6] in addition to writing Adventist mission history.[7]

To reflect on Seventh-day Adventist Missiology means to consider the historical patterns of the expansion of the church and their theological background as well as present-day issues. Some insight can be gained if theological, strategical, and practical dimensions of Adventist mission are compared particularly with the evangelical movement, for Adventists have more affinity with evangelicals than with any other major block of contemporary Christianity.

---

[5] E.g., W. Mueller, *Der Dienst der Mission*, Hamburg: Vollmer & Bentlin, 1940.

[6] The following publications may serve as examples: Ernst Kotz, *Im Banne der Furcht: Sitten und Gebräuche der Wapare in Ostafrika*, AV, [1922]; Ernst Kotz., *Grammatik des Chasu in Deutsch-Ostafrika (Pare-Gebirge)*, Berlin: Reimer, 1909.

[7] Many SDA church histories have a focus on mission or portray SDA church history as mission history: John N. Loughborough, *Rise and Progress of the Seventh-Day Adventists*, Battle Creek: General Conference Association of Seventh-day Adventists, 1892; William A. Spicer, *Our Story of Missions*, PPPA, 1921; M.E. Olsen, *Origin and Progress of Seventh-Day Adventists*, RHPA, 1925; Wesley Amundsen, *The Advent Message in Inter-America*, RHPA, 1947; Mervyn C. Maxwell, *Tell it to the World: The Story of Seventh-Day Adventists*, PPPA, 1977.

Chapter 1

The Historical Development of Adventist Mission and Underlying Theological Emphases

During the last 25 years, various attempts have been made to periodize Adventist history from a missiological perspective.[1] In these, it has been recognized that the expansion of the Seventh-day Adventist Church reflects a missiological development that starts with a - theologically as well as geographically - rather narrow view of the task the movement is given and then gradually widens its focus making the church advance throughout the world. Thus, even the overall history of Seventh-day Adventism can be understood as the history of this church's developing mission.

In this study, I will take Jesus' words in Acts 1:8 as an analogy to the historical stages that the Adventist Church has gone through: "You will be my witnesses in Jerusalem, and in all Judea and Samaria, and to the ends of the earth." (NIV) As the early Christian Church spread step by step, crossing geographical and cultural borders only after some initial reluctance, Seventh-day Adventism, too, took some time to reach out beyond the narrow confines of its own Jerusalem and Judea as well as to emerge with a theology that would demand to widen this limited focus.

---

[1] Borge Schantz, "Development of SDA Missionary Thought", 1983, pp. 199-446, presents the following periodization: The American Experience (1830-1860) - The Christendom Experience (1860-1890); The World-Wide Experience I (1890-1900); II (1900-1940); III (starting 1940). Gottfried Oosterwal, in *Mission: Possible*, SPA, 1972, p. 23-41, distinguishes 4 phases: the "Shut-Door period" (1844-1850s); the phase when work amongst other churches in America was started (1850s-1874), the time after the first official missionary was sent out from North America (1874-1950s), and a last period that focuses on the formerly unreached non-Christian peoples (starting in the 1950s).

Birth Pangs: The Millerite Movement, 1831-1844

Most missionary movements have their roots in revivals.[2] Similar to other missionary movements, Seventh-day Adventism emerged from a mid-19th century revival movement – the American Millerite Movement. It is a young denomination that draws reasons for its existence from a specific interpretation of this historical background: the Millerite Movement with its emphasis on the imminent second coming of Jesus has usually been interpreted by Seventh-day Adventists as God's hand in history.[3] Indeed, there is historical continuity between both the histories and the missiologies of the short-lived Millerite Revival and the only church organization resulting from it that has continued growing significantly until present.

William Miller (1782-1849) and his associates, preachers and lay people of different Protestant denominations in the United States of America, derived their message from a study of prophecy that led them to the issue of time elements in the books of Daniel and Revelation.[4] Linking these to the "blessed hope" of the second coming of Jesus gave their proclamation a sense of urgency that was clearly different from the postmillennial persuasions of many of North America's clergy who believed that human progress will prepare the establishment of the Kingdom of God on earth.[5] Millerite premillennial

---

[2] Klaus Fiedler, *The Story of Faith Missions*, Oxford: Regnum, 1994, p. 13.

[3] Denominational church histories strongly emphasize those aspects of the Millerite Movement which are more favourable, for example those that contributed to the development of the SDA Church; see, e.g. Richard W. Schwarz, *Light Bearers to the Remnant*, PPPA, 1979, pp. 24-71; George R. Knight, *A Brief History of Seventh-Day Adventists*, RHPA, 1999, pp. 13-27.

[4] They formed part of a larger movement which Fiedler calls the "Prophetic movement" which was pre-millennial, see Fiedler, *The Story of Faith Missions*, pp. 272-279.

[5] On the differences between post- and premillennialism and their impact on missionary movements, see Klaus Fiedler, "Shifts in Eschatology - Shifts in Missiology", in Jochen Eber (ed.), *Hope does not Disappoint: Studies in Eschatology. Essays from Different Contexts*, Wheaton: World Evangelical Fellowship; Bangalore: Theological Book Trust, 2001, pp. 163-186.

eschatology, on the other hand, emphasized the need for repentance and preparation for the coming King.[6]

The mission of Millerism was not to preach the gospel to the world but to prepare people for the end. Miller and his fellow preachers believed that the progress made by missionary societies was a proof that the Great Commission of Matthew 28:18-20 and the prophecies of Matthew 24:14 and Revelation 14:6-7 had been fulfilled: "The Gospel has now spread over the four quarters of the globe", was their conviction.[7] Thus, what the Millerites thought remained to be done was to warn the world of the imminent coming; this, according to one of the leaders of the movement, Josiah Litch, had been accomplished in 1843.[8] In fact, by then the movement's leading periodicals, *Signs of the Times* and *Midnight Cry* as well as tracts and other publications had been sent into most of the places inhabited by Christians World-Wide, including missionary stations. A shortcoming of this literature work, however, was the fact that it was mostly English that was used.[9]

Millerism had a mission, but in spite of its tremendous evangelistic activities,[10] the movement did not develop a concept of mission that went beyond proclaiming the near advent to those who would listen. As an apocalyptic intra-Christian revival movement based in the Northern states of the USA, it did not claim to contribute to either missions or the reflection on it - rather, leading proponents of Millerism saw the movement as a climax of all Christian mission that would lead to its end and fulfillment. The fulfillment hoped for, however, did not come, and this made the movement to end instead of the world.

---

[6] George Knight, *Millennial Fever and the End of the World: A Study of Millerite Adventism*, PPPA, 1993.

[7] William Miller, "A Lecture on the Signs of the Present Times", *Signs of the Times*, March 20, 1840, p. 4, quoted in Damsteegt, *Foundations of the SDA Message and Mission*, p. 50.

[8] *Ibid.*, p. 52.

[9] *Ibid.*, p. 54. Many countries are mentioned; publications were sent to "nearly all English and American missionary stations on the earth"; however, no translation work is referred to here.

[10] An estimated 500,000 people attended the movement's camp meetings from 1842 to 1844 according to Schwarz, *Light Bearers*, p. 41; Miller had given 3200 lectures between 1832 and 1844 (*ibid.*, p. 48).

Jerusalem: The "Shut Door", 1844-1850

For the emerging sabbatarian Adventist group remaining from the "Great Disappointment" of 1844,[11] its early years of existence did not allow a mission among non-Millerites.[12] The "Shut-Door"-theory held by many of the post-1844 Adventists including the sabbatarians considered all those who did not believe in the messages preached by the Millerites as "fallen"; they presumed that "the door [of grace] was shut" for all who had not loved the coming of the Savior.[13] As the opportunity to repent was over for most of the earth's inhabitants, so they believed, it was only a matter of persevering until the Lord would come to take home his few elect who were faithful, continuing to believe in his soon appearance.[14]

While, during more than a decade after 1844, the hope was strong that it was only a matter of weeks or months until they were going to heaven,[15] much time was spent in Bible study by the future Seventh-day Adventists, carving out a set of beliefs that would provide a basis

---

[11] The Millerites first - in the 1830s and early 1840s - expected Jesus to return very soon, but without a specific date; but their speculative calculations based on Daniel 8:14 led most of them to accept first the year 1843 and then October 22, 1844, as the day for the *parousia*. When this hope was not fulfilled, this date became synonymous with the "Great Disappointment" that the Millerites experienced.

[12] George R. Knight, "From Shut Door to Worldwide Mission: The Dynamic Context of Early German Adventism", in Baldur Ed. Pfeiffer et al., *Die Adventisten und Hamburg*, Frankfurt: Lang, 1992, p. 47, even calls this period the time of "the Antimission People".

[13] Schwarz, *Light Bearers*, pp. 55, 69, 70; for the impact on Seventh-day Adventists, see Rolf J. Pöhler, "'And the Door was Shut' - Seventh-Day Adventists and the Shut-Door Doctrine in the Decade after the Great Disappointment", unpubl. paper, AU, 1978.

[14] Rolf J. Pöhler, "Change in Seventh-Day Adventist Theology: A Study of the Problem of Doctrinal Development", ThD, AU, 1995, pp. 228-233 (the section, "Coping with the delay").

[15] Ibid., p. 228. James and Ellen White even encouraged people to hold on in faith "a few more days"; see *A Word to the "Little Flock"*, p. 8, Brunswick, Maine: by the authors, 1847. Furthermore, some leaders of sabbatarian Adventists like Bates continued to set new dates for the advent going up to 1851; see Schwarz, *Light Bearers*, p. 66.

for drawing together those individuals remaining from the 1844 revival who were open to join a new movement. The primary mission of early sabbatarian Adventism was thus to build a foundation for a future church by stabilizing itself doctrinally and in terms of adherents.[16] The first "mission field" of the emerging Seventh-day Adventist movement were the Millerites. Methods similar to those used by the movement before 1844 were used: preaching, publications, and Bible conferences.[17] Like Jesus' disciples who waited for Pentecost, early sabbatarian Adventists did not reach out beyond their own Jerusalem.

Judea: White North America, 1850-1870

The new truths agreed upon in a number of "Sabbath Conferences" from 1848 onwards - the Sabbath doctrine, the teaching on the heavenly sanctuary, and a few others, such as the mortality of the soul - as well as the dynamic personalities who met each other in this melting pot of beliefs, ideas, and backgrounds, were like yeast working through a dough of group identity that grew in sabbatarian Adventism in the 1850s and made it increase in terms of numbers, too. This can be shown by its growth from less than 100 persons in 1849 to 250 in 1852 and 3500 in the founding year of the church organization, 1863.[18]

The beginning of the 1850s marks a new period in SDA Missiology. Already in the summer of 1849, James White, the unofficial leader of the movement for many years, started the first paper of sabbatarian Adventists, *Present Truth*, published "in defense of the truth". Then, in 1850, *Present Truth* and a second new project of White, *Advent Review*, were replaced by *Second Advent Review and Sabbath Her-*

---

[16] Schantz, "Development of SDA Missionary Thought", pp. 199-236, tends to downplay the limited missionary vision in the stages of Millerism and early post-1844 years and to project the later thoroughly missionary attitude of the church into these foundational years. A good explanation, however, for the "Shut-Door" period of little mission activity provided here, however, is that it was a time "to come to deep agreement as to their essential mission" (p. 218).
[17] Schwarz, *Light Bearers*, 67-85.
[18] Don F. Neufeld (ed.), *SDA Encyclopedia*, RHPA, 1976, p. 1167.

ald.[19] Thus, the idea of merely persevering without missionary activities was slowly replaced by the need of interacting with a greater public: North America became Adventism's Judea.

In 1852, one of the most important sabbatarian figures, Joseph Bates, abandoned his shut-door beliefs when he found that the Presbyterian David Hewitt responded to his preaching on the Sabbath almost immediately. Hewitt, who lived in Battle Creek which should soon become the centre of Seventh-day Adventism, had not been touched by Millerite Adventism before.[20] As the focal point of Adventism moved from the American East to the Midwest and work was later opened even in California (1868), the movement was confronted with many more people who had not been exposed to Millerism that was centred more on the East Coast.

Still, opposition to a larger mission existed among the emerging Seventh-day Adventist Church. In the end of the 1850s, Uriah Smith, editor of *Review and Herald* from 1855, opposed investing in foreign missions as long as there were poor people at home, and M.E. Cornell, one of the most prominent early SDA evangelists, considered it futile to serve in countries where Christianity was not welcomed.[21]

However, an important step towards a missionary identity and a growing missiological reflection was the question of church organization in the late 1850s and early 1860s. It was in connection with the conflict over the necessity of a formally organized church and the question whether organization was permitted by the Bible that Seventh-day Adventists decided that the reason for their existence was to reach out. The name adopted by the young denomination, Seventh-day Adventist Church, was to describe two elements of its initial mission: to continue proclaiming the near advent of Jesus Christ and to present a major new doctrine to the world - the seventh-day Sabbath as a binding commandment for Christians.

---

[19] This magazine continues to be published up to the present as *Adventist Review*; Schwarz, *Light Bearers*, p. 74-76.
[20] *Ibid.*, p. 80.
[21] RH, April 24, 1856, pp. 11-12; August 19, 1858, p. 105; RH, December 22, 1859, p. 37; quoted in Schantz, "Development of SDA Missionary Thought", p. 233.

For almost another decade after coming up with a denominational organization, North America was seen as a sufficient field for the mission of the church.[22] Uriah Smith argued that through immigrants, the peoples of the world were assembled in it and thus the mission of the Seventh-day Adventist Church could be fulfilled there.[23] Likewise, when in 1868, a "Vigilant Mission Society" was set up by Stephen Haskell, its aims were not cross-national or cross-cultural mission but mainly to promote personal evangelism by church members in the USA.[24]

Samaria: The Christian World, 1870-1890

A change in missionary activity and concepts was brought about when more and more Americans of immediate European origin became Adventists who were still much attached to their home country and culture. They naturally did not believe in proclaiming the message only in "Judea" but saw the need of spreading it amongst their peoples on the other side of the ocean. Thus, in 1872, still in North America, the denomination started to produce the first of its foreign language periodicals in Danish, *Advent Tidende*; others in French, German, Norwegian, and Swedish followed soon. These papers were an important step of Adventist mission into Christendom outside the "new world". These missionary activities were managed by the "Missionary Society of Seventh-day Adventists" that was founded already in mid-1869 but confined its activities initially mainly to literature work - although sending out missionaries was one of its objectives, too.[25]

---

[22] The first conference of churches was formed in 1861 in Michigan, and the General Conference, a governing body of all conferences, in 1863; see George R. Knight, *A Brief History of Seventh-Day Adventists*, RHPA, 1999, p. 63. Canada was entered in 1862; see Schantz, "Development of SDA Missionary Thought", p. 775.
[23] RH, May 27, 1858, p. 13; February 3, 1859, p. 87, quoted in Schantz, "Development of SDA Missionary Thought", p. 239.
[24] Schwarz, *Light Bearers*, p. 152.
[25] Schantz, "Development of SDA Missionary Thought", p. 365.

James White had expressed the idea of sending a worker to Europe as early as 1862, but the general climate of the early 1860s did not yet seem favourable for the church to start a missionary thrust towards Europe. When the General Conference denied to send Michael B. Czechowski, a 1857 convert and successful evangelist particularly amongst immigrants in the USA, as a missionary to Europe in 1864,[26] he decided to go there under the auspices of a non-sabbatarian Adventist group. Reaching Europe, he still preached the Sabbath while concealing his links to the Seventh-day Adventist Church, an activity that later led to first contacts of Swiss and Romanian individuals to the General Conference.[27]

Ten years later, the situation had changed. The General Conference sent its first official missionary, John N. Andrews who had been its president from 1867-1869, to Switzerland. Unfortunately, his success was very limited as he confined his activities almost entirely to editing literature; thus, he was not able to establish a thriving church.[28]

More outstanding attempts of missionary endeavour than Czechowski's self-made mission and Andrews' hardly contextualized approach were made by the Dane Jan G. Matteson and the German Ludwig R. Conradi. They went back to their home countries in 1877 and 1886, respectively, planting many churches and developing a European SDA identity in spite of resistance of state churches. Conradi developed the strategy to win converts from Baptist background first in various places, then more and more from Lutheran and Catholic areas, organizing the church also among German emigrants in Russia and other Eastern European countries.[29] Similar efforts were undertaken by Seventh-day Adventists among the white population of Southern Africa from 1887 onwards and in Australia starting in 1885.

---

[26] The reasons stated by the church leaders were his lacking ability to handle finances and his too independent personality; see Schwarz, *Light Bearers*, p. 142.
[27] *Ibid*, pp. 143-144.
[28] Daniel Heinz, "L.R. Conradis missionarischer Durchbruch: Ein Modell für die Zukunft?", in Pfeiffer et al., *Die Adventisten und Hamburg*, p. 148.
[29] Schwarz, *Light Bearers*, pp. 217-220.

In this period, there was a growing awareness that the Seventh-day Adventist message was to be spread to all Christians in the world.[30] One of the church's strongest mission advocates, Ellen G. White, visited Europe from 1885-1887[31] and settled in Australia for one decade, 1891-1900, practically and thus participated actively in serving on the cutting edge of the church's mission during this stage.

Another new field entered during this time was the South of the USA. Formerly rejected there because of their abolitionist views, Seventh-day Adventists slowly started to work particularly among Blacks. There were a few attempts in the 1870s and 80s, but it was only in 1893 that James Edson White, son of Ellen and James White, began to apply considerable effort for the Afro-Americans.[32] There was a similar geographical distance to the centre of Adventism as the American West; however, the differences of lifestyle, values, and background between the South and the North as well as between Blacks and Whites made this project a more significant cross-cultural mission project of the church.

The World: The Everlasting Gospel to all Nations

Around the early 1890s, the persuasion came up among Seventh-day Adventists that the church has a mission for the whole world, even the non-Christians. More than the rather symbolic mission on famous Pitcairn Island, enthusiastically promoted by the General Conference in 1890,[33] it were visionary leaders like Ellen White who made it clear that now the time had come for an Adventist outreach beyond Christian countries. Being in Australia in 1892, she wrote:

---

[30] Apart from the countries mentioned, the following were entered during this period: 1876: France; 1877: Italy; 1878: Norway, England; 1880: Sweden; 1886: New Zealand, Russia; 1888: Poland; 1889: Holland, Turkey (Armenians); see Schantz, "Development of SDA Missionary Thought", pp. 775-777.
[31] Her husband had died in 1881.
[32] Schwarz, *Light Bearers*, pp. 233-249; Ronald Graybill, *Mission to Black America*, PPPA, 1971, passim.
[33] Schwarz, *Light Bearers*, pp. 222-223.

The missionary work in Australia and New Zealand is yet in its infancy; but the same work must be accomplished in Australia, New Zealand, in Africa, India, China, and the islands of the sea, as have been accomplished in the home field.[34]

Already in 1886, General Conference president George I. Butler came up with the idea that the Christian countries being reached at the moment must become springboards for further expansion:

> every true Seventh-day Adventist must be interested in the welfare of our leading missions which are organized and sustained to send the light to the regions beyond.[35]

Thus, in the 1890s and the first decades of the 20th century, more and more countries without any Christian background were targeted.[36] Seventh-day Adventists recognized that the USA had been reached with their message to a considerable extent and that the time to reach the formerly unreached countries of Africa, South America, the Pacific, and Asia had come. Whereas Adventist mission before this period was more like a random exercise that consisted in responding to calls from outside, it is at this time that one can recognize the emergence of a mission strategy: in 1889, the newly formed "Foreign Mission Board" began its work with a full-time secretary, and S.N. Haskell, one of the pioneer leaders of Adventism, made a world tour on its behalf in the same year.[37]

Much of this missionary expansion was due to apt church leadership. Arthur G. Daniells, after being a missionary in New Zealand and Australia for 13 years, became the church's world leader in 1901 dur-

---

[34] *Fundamentals of Christian Education*, SPA, 1923, pp. 208-209.
[35] RH, October 5, 1886, p. 616.
[36] Some of the new fields were also predominantly Catholic countries: 1890: Argentina 1891: Honduras; 1892: Nicaragua; other countries included (with emphasis on Africa) 1894: Chile, Ghana, Zimbabwe; 1895: Fiji, Samoa, Tonga; 1896: Japan; 1899: Egypt, Lesotho; 1900: Indonesia; 1901: Jordan; 1902: Malawi, Burma, China; 1903: Tanzania, Spain, Cuba; etc. 1905: Algeria, Zambia; 1906: Kenya; 1907: Ethiopia; 1914: Nigeria, Mauritius; 1920: Swaziland, Rwanda, Zaire; 1921: Botswana; 1924: Angola; 1925: Burundi, Morocco; 1926: Cameroon, Liberia, Madagascar, Uganda; 1928: Tunisia (Schantz, "Development of SDA Missionary Thought", pp. 777-779).
[37] Schantz, "Development of SDA Missionary Thought", pp. 332-333, 375.

ing a General Conference session that effected, under his guidance, fundamental changes in the worldwide church structure which made it to function like a big missionary society. The General Conference committee, the highest authority in church administration, was assigned the task to direct the world mission of the church. With Daniells as a dynamic leader and the equally mission-minded William A. Spicer, former missionary to England and India, as secretary, three mission decades followed.[38] While world mission used to be an option or just one function of the church before, it became its heartbeat after 1901. Spicer argued in this period:

> The cause of world wide missions is not something in addition to the regular work of the church. The work of God is one work the wide world over. The Gospel message can never have accomplished its purpose until it has reached all lands.[39]

Daniells was a mission strategist. He put into practice the "springboard plan" of investing into fields that could soon be self-supporting and send missionaries, too. Under his leadership during 20 years, missionaries sent out annually were almost 100 as compared to an average of 5 before, reaching 700 North American SDA missionaries in 1918 and 1200 in 1935 - 6.5% and 9.9% [!] of all American Protestant missionaries, respectively.[40]

It was not only from the USA that missionaries were sent out and new territories were entered. Many European Adventists were sent into their nations' colonies and started missions there as early as the first decade of the 20th century, e.g. in Kenya, Tanzania, and Algeria. Others "adopted" countries, such as the Scandinavian Seventh-day Adventists who chose Ethiopia as their mission field. Australians reached out into the Pacific, and from South Africa, Zimbabwe and Zambia were reached. The "springboard plan" worked well.

---

[38] Spicer and Daniells exchanged positions in 1922.
[39] William A. Spicer, *Our Story of Missions*, PPPA, 1921, p. 11.
[40] Robert T. Coote, "Twentieth-Century Shifts in the North American Protestant Missionary Community", *International Bulletin of Missionary Research*, Vol. 22/4 (1998), pp. 152-153; the total number of all American Protestant missionaries was 10,800 in 1918 and 12100 in 1935 according to Coote.

An important theological background for this new missionary and missiological stage was the famous 1888 General Conference Session of Minneapolis. There, a major correction in theological emphasis took place - again, under the guidance of Ellen G. White, but also through young proponents of a new prioritization in soteriology, Alonzo T. Jones and Ellet J. Waggoner. They emphasized that all distinctive Seventh-day Adventist doctrines are not valuable without, and should be subject to, the centre of the gospel - righteousness by faith.[41] Although this new weight on the cross as against the traditional Seventh-day Adventist emphasis on the law was rejected by many at the conference meeting, in the following years, the "1888 message" did not only become a ferment of spiritual renewal of Adventist leadership but also provided a framework for a Missiology that would postulate the need for outreach to heathen lands. Adventism was now no more exclusively a reform movement promoting its distinctives in a Christian context but a church with the task of bringing basic Christian teachings – the gospel – to those outside Christianity. Revelation 14:6-12, the call of the angel to all nations, tongues, and peoples which the Seventh-day Adventist Church has persistently interpreted as being related to its own history, was begun to be understood in a fuller light. Adventism, while continuing to view mission mainly as an "invitation to join the eschatological community",[42] started to realize that many more had to be invited than it had been formerly believed.

The Ends of the Earth: Global Mission and the Unreached

Almost one hundred years of world mission brought into existence Seventh-day Adventist churches in most countries of the world[43] but

---

[41] Schwarz, *Light Bearers*, 183-197.
[42] David J. Bosch, *Transforming Mission: Paradigm Shifts in Theology of Mission*, Maryknoll: Orbis, 1991, p. 123.
[43] Major countries not entered in 1993 were: Afghanistan, Bhutan, Comoros, Djibouti, Libya, Mauritania, Oman, Palestine, Qatar, Saudi Arabia, Somalia, Syria, Tunisia, Western Sahara, and Yemen; in addition to them, some tiny countries such as Andorra, Liechtenstein, and Monaco. However, there is a considerable number of countries with fewer than 50 members consisting sometimes of mainly mission

still left nearly half of the world population untouched – and even unreachable - with its message. After World War II, the missionary concept of the church, as that of many other missions, was to continue the pre-war mission and simply expand its activities in the fields where missions had been planted already. Then, when independence came in most African and Asian nations, it phased out foreign, mostly American, leadership in order to allow nationals to take over. With the handing over of responsibility on all levels, the world church also assigned unentered territories to the Division[44] they are in, leaving the task of reaching the formerly unreached in existing Adventist fields with the country-wide or regional administrative units. However, because of financial constraints, a large number of growing institutions to be supported, and regional/ethnic concentrations of church membership, outreach into new areas has often not been easy. Throughout the 20th century, there has been no SDA foreign mission department at the General Conference level which was a strength in the beginning of the century, involving the world church leadership directly into its world mission. This, however, became a weakness when all reachable countries were reached, giving leadership the impression that their task was done.[45] Thus, in spite of the establishment of an orientation course for missionaries in 1966 and the creation of a Department of World Mission at Andrews University in the same

---

personnel or expatriates: Algeria, Bahrain, Brunei, Congo, Cyprus, Iran, Laos, Maledives, Malta, Morocco, Mongolia, Niger, Oman, Turkey, Turkmenistan. Other countries that have below 500 Seventh-day Adventists are: Albania, Armenia, Azerbaijan, Burkina Faso, Cambodia, Gambia, Georgia, Guinea, Guinea-Bissau, Iraq, Israel, Jordan, Kuwait, Macedonia, Mali, Nepal, Senegal, Slovenia, Tajikistan, United Arab Emirates (62!). See "131st Annual Statistical Report - 1993", Silver Spring: General Conference of Seventh-day Adventists, 1994, pp. 42-42.

[44] The currently 12 Divisions are the largest administrative unit below the General Conference, usually comprising a continent or a major part of it.

[45] This structural problem is what Bruce L. Bauer deplores in "Structure and Mission", in Dybdahl, *Adventist Mission in the 21st Century*, pp. 159-166. He demands that an Adventist missionary society or a department of mission be established in order to revive the missionary spirit in the denomination.

year,[46] there was a sharp decline in the number of Adventist missionaries, particularly from North America, although financial and membership growth continued in the same period.[47] There has been a "gradual slowing of the outward missionary thrust from homeland churches", as Russell Staples, one of the leading Seventh-day Adventist missiologists puts it, reasoning that it may be the very success of the mission thrust of earlier decades that shifted not only the weight in membership but also the belief about who is responsible for accomplishing the mission of the church from Europe and America to the Two-Thirds World.[48]

It is only recently that the General Conference readjusted this mission philosophy. Apart from similar trends in other evangelical missions and denominations,[49] it were again insights derived from the Biblical passage so important to the Seventh-day Adventist Church, Revelation 14:6,[50] that led church leaders to de-emphasize countries reached and to focus on smaller units. In 1986, the General Conference voted *Global Mission*, an initiative that aims at establishing an SDA presence in every population segment of 1 million persons in the world. Starting to be implemented in 1990, 2300 such unreached seg-

---

[46] Gottfried Oosterwal, "Training for Missions Tomorrow", in Dunton et al., *Adventist Missions Facing the 21st Century*, pp. 78-91; Gottfried Oosterwal, "Mission Institute Reaches 20th year", AR, Vol. 137 (26 June 1986), pp. 20-22.

[47] In 1968, there were around 1500 North American SDA missionaries; in 1996, around 700 were left according to Coote, "Twentieth-century Shifts in the North American Protestant Missionary Community", pp. 152-153. The positive side of the coin is the internationalization of these SDA "regular" missionaries (today called Inter-Division Employees); according to Pat Gustin, current Director of the Institute of World Mission of the SDA Church, more than half of SDA Inter-Division Employees come from outside North America [personal interview, Nairobi, April 1999], the largest part of them from the Philippines.

[48] Russell Staples, "Maintaining the Adventist Vision", in Baumgartner, *Re-Visioning Adventist Mission in Europe*, p. 4.

[49] Compare e.g. the focus on the unreached in Patrick Johnstone, *Operation World*, 5th rev. ed., Carlisle: OM, 1993, p. 21 and passim as well as "The 10/40 Window", Colorado Springs: The AD 2000 & Beyond Movement, n.d.

[50] "Then I saw another angel flying in midair, and he had the eternal gospel to proclaim to those who live on the earth - to every nation, tribe, language, and people." (NIV)

ments were identified that were then targeted with different strategies, one of the main tools being *Global Mission Pioneers*, volunteers who know the local situation and work as church planters for a small stipend. Through this global plan, 500 of the 2300 segments were reached until 1995.[51] In spite of very little training of the volunteers and sometimes rather short periods of service financed by the General Conference that sometimes led to interrupted or discontinued projects, this initiative shows that there is both a need and willingness to reach beyond the areas and groups of people where the church has been established. Meanwhile, one important correction has also been applied on the *Global Mission* plans: the 1 million people segments have proved to be still far too big, and in some areas, smaller units have been established. As time goes by, knowledge about more and more ethnic, social, cultural, and economic people groups will emerge. The unreached have come back into the focus of Adventist mission![52]

Besides the *Global Mission* initiative, various new Adventist mission organizations have been established during the last two decades. *Adventist Frontier Missions*[53] for example is an organization sending out long-term missionaries into unreached people groups around the world. According to its example, *Philippine Frontier Missions* and *Myanmar Frontier Missions* have been founded by Adventists in the respective countries, targeting mainly people groups in their own lands. Other initiatives include the Student Missionary program in which mainly American college students have gone to assist in various projects since the 1960s, averaging more than 300 per year in the 80s

---

[51] "Intentional Outreach", Interview with Michael Ryan [Global Mission Coordinator at the GC], AR 172/23 (June 8, 1995), pp. 10-11; Charles R. Taylor [Director of Research and Statistics for Global Mission], "Measuring a Dream", ibid., p. 8; Mike L. Ryan, "Global Mission Reaches Out", in Dybdahl, *Adventist Mission in the 21st Century*, pp. 286-290.

[52] Bruce Campbell Moyer, "The Unreached People: Mission as Maintenance or Opening New Frontiers", in Dunton et al., *Adventist Missions Facing the 21st Century*, pp. 38-52.

[53] Cathy E. Morgan, "A Case Study: Adventist Frontier Mission", in Dybdahl, *Adventist Mission in the 21st Century*, pp. 255-262.

and 90s.⁵⁴ Moreover, through the *1000 Missionary Movement*, a student/volunteer program similarly designed for one-year projects, Eastern Asian Seventh-day Adventists have sent more than 1000 young people to more or less unreached areas in their own territory in the 1990s.⁵⁵

Another crucial feature of recent Adventist missiological developments is the adoption of a mission statement by the General Conference. Interestingly, it includes different aspects of mission: preaching, teaching, and healing. Both the central Christian message, the gospel as shared with other Christians, and the particular Seventh-day Adventist emphasis on Revelation 14:6-12 are included in the statement.⁵⁶

Apart from the mentioned developments of geographical missionary expansion, there have been coming up, particularly during the last few decades, new issues and phenomena that will be treated in the following sections.

---

⁵⁴ Pat Gustin, "Student Missionaries and Volunteers", in Baumgartner, *Re-Visioning Adventist Mission in Europe*, p. 161; Pat Gustin, "Student Missions – An Army of Youth", in Dybdahl, *Adventist Mission in the 21st Century*, pp. 174-181.
⁵⁵ *Maranatha*, Vol. 7/1 (January-February 1998), p. 4; G.T. Ng, "Reaching Asia: The 1000 Missionary Movement", in Dybdahl, *Adventist Mission in the 21st Century*, pp. 248-254.
⁵⁶ The SDA Mission Statement is found in the *General Conference Working Policy* (1998-1999 edition), p. 27, and is fully rendered in Appendix I.

Chapter 2

Systematic Aspects

Seventh-day Adventist Missiology – an Evangelical Missiology?

Seventh-day Adventist Missiology is evangelical in most of its aspects, and the Seventh-day Adventist Church can be understood as part of the evangelical movement. This is evident when considering the historical origin of Adventism which was fuelled strongly by Methodist and Baptist elements. Furthermore, there have been friendly contacts with other evangelical churches especially since the Seventh-day Adventist Church entered its World Mission period. For instance, there has been an active participation in the 1910 Edinburgh World Mission Conference and the acceptance of comity agreements in some cases in the beginning of SDA mission activities in non-Christian lands.[1] Adventism's evangelical character can also be seen when one reviews important evangelical missiological declarations such as the *Lausanne Covenant*[2] and compares them with the *27 Fundamental Beliefs* of Seventh-day Adventists[3] and other Adventist statements and publications that deal with the mission of the church as well as Ellen G. White's writings.

Seventh-day Adventists will agree whole-heartedly with almost all of the articles of the *Lausanne Covenant*. With it, they believe that God is a missionary God who wants His people to be builders of His kingdom, they uphold the authority of the Bible, calling it infallible,

---

[1] Schantz, "Development of SDA Missionary Thought", pp. 287-393.
[2] John Stott (ed.), *Making Christ Known: Historic Mission Documents from the Lausanne Movement, 1974-1989*, Carlisle: Paternoster, 1996, pp. 1-55.
[3] *Seventh-Day Adventists Believe...: A Biblical Exposition of 27 Fundamental Doctrines*, Silver Spring: Ministerial Association of the General Conference of Seventh-day Adventists, 1988.

and they believe that Christ is the only and universal Saviour of mankind.[4] They also agree with the statements made about the nature of evangelism and Christian social responsibility that carefully balance these two aspects of Christian mission while putting more weight on evangelistic witness.[5] There is a difference, however, in that SDA Church policy and tradition discourages active political participation especially for its employees[6] whereas the *Lausanne Covenant* makes "socio-political involvement ... part of our Christian duty", but shows that this responsibility is not to be equated with evangelism.[7]

Adventists would subscribe to some of the ideas of the sections on the Church and evangelism and co-operation in evangelism,[8] especially the centrality of the evangelistic task and its being the *raison d'être* for the existence of the church as well as the need for strategic planning. However, the Seventh-day Adventist Church has always been very cautious concerning the question of co-operation. In spite of recognizing "those agencies that lift up Christ before men as a part of the divine plan for evangelization of the world",[9] most Seventh-day Adventists have always felt that they cannot directly co-operate with non-sabbatarian churches, not even with those evangelical groups that are very close to them theologically and in Christian lifestyle.[10] Because of its focus on specific doctrines, the Seventh-day Adventist Church makes unity in outreach dependent on acceptance of its theol-

---

[4] Articles 1-3 of the Lausanne Covenant; see Stott, *Making Christ Known*, p. 9, 13, 16; *Seventh-Day Adventists Believe*, p. 5-57; 106-117 (articles about the Holy Scriptures, the Godhead, God the Father, and Jesus Christ).

[5] Articles 4-5; see Stott, *Making Christ Known*, p. 20, 24.

[6] *Working Policy of the General Conference of Seventh-Day Adventists: 1995-1996 Edition*, RHPA, 1995, p. 312 (section HA 15 on ADRA) and 482 (section S 50 on Conflict of Interest). Particularly for SDA pastors, there was traditionally a clear although unwritten rule of political non-involvement. The "Conflict of Interest" section, although not stating this, is a parallel concerning business activities.

[7] Stott, *Making Christ Known*, p. 24.

[8] Articles 6-7; *ibid.*, p. 28.

[9] See section O 75 (Relationships with Other Christian Churches and Religious Organizations) of the *Working Policy 1995-1996*, p. 401.

[10] E.g., Seventh-day Adventists use much evangelical literature in evangelism (like Bill Bright's "Four Spiritual Laws"), apologetics (e.g. in creationism or biblical historicity questions), and church life (e.g., contemporary song books).

ogy. Therefore, the Adventists agree with the Lausanne movement that "Organizational unity may take many forms and does not necessarily forward evangelism" but do not support the idea that a closer unity of all evangelicals will bring forth the accomplishment of world evangelization. Rather, many Adventists, supporting their views by prophetic statements of Ellen White, continue to expect that the difficulties experienced by Adventism in 19th century America because of evangelicals pushing for a national Sunday law will be repeated on a global scale, leading to a persecution of Adventists and ushering in the closing chapters of earth's history.[11] Thus, at large, Adventism is rather a "loner" in its missionary outreach, not being a member in any of the significant evangelical or interdenominational organizations except in certain obvious areas of Christian co-operation such as the Bible Societies or relief and development.

However, together with the Lausanne Movement, Adventism believes in evangelistic partnership with churches in the Two-Thirds World - in the case of Adventism, partnership with its World Divisions - especially in view of the urgency of the evangelistic task of reaching the unreached billions of people. Therefore, continuing to send missionaries not only from the USA and Europe but from everywhere to everywhere is one of its policies.[12] Although there are no official statements about culture and the gospel in the view of the Seventh-day Adventist Church,[13] Lausanne's balanced view of evangelism and culture presenting the need of contextualization while cautioning that every culture contains demonic elements would be accepted by most Adventist leaders. Similarly, the article on education and leadership that stresses nurture, indigenization, and thorough Bible-based

---

[11] White, *The Great Controversy*, pp. 563-592; G. Edward Reid, *Sunday's Coming: Eye-Opening Evidence that These Are the Very Last Days*, by the author, 1996 [Reid is the Stewardship Director of the North American Division of Seventh-day Adventists].

[12] Articles 8-9; see Stott, *Making Christ Known*, p. 33; cf. section C 65 10 (From Everywhere to Everywhere) of the *Working Policy 1995-1996*, pp. 86-87, that says that the "ever-expanding world mission program" of the SDA Church continues to need missionaries going in and coming from all directions.

[13] But see section 4.5 on culture and contextualization in this study.

theological education that is at the same time evangelism-oriented, speaks about an important concern of the denomination today.[14]

Furthermore, Seventh-day Adventists know about the spiritual nature of the conflict that the church faces while in its mission,[15] and about persecution that may arise from the proclamation of the gospel; they also fully support liberty of conscience.[16] Adventists share the belief that it is only through the power of the Holy Spirit that worldwide evangelization can be accomplished[17] and that "Jesus Christ will return personally and visibly, in power and glory, to consummate his salvation and his judgment", rejecting the idea of an earthly utopia. They likewise believe that before the *parousia*, "the Gospel must first be preached to all nations".[18]

Altogether, it is surely not overstated that Seventh-day Adventists belong to the larger picture of the evangelical movement. Even if not closely connected to official networks of evangelicals, theological affinities and similarities of (mainly missionary!) activity make Adventists resemble evangelicals of other backgrounds.[19]

---

[14] Articles 10-11; *ibid.*, p. 39.
[15] Article 12; see Stott, *Making Christ Known*, p. 44; cf. the section about the "Great Controversy" in *Seventh-Day Adventists Believe*, pp. 98-105, as well as Ellen White, *Great Controversy*, passim.
[16] Article 13; see Stott, *Making Christ Known*, p. 44. The SDA Church even encourages its own members who do not agree with its principles to be free to leave the church; see *Working Policy 1995-1996*, p. 402.
[17] Article 14; see Stott, *Making Christ Known*, p. 49; SDA eschatology talks about the "latter rain", a time during which a special outpouring of the Holy Spirit is expected; see e.g. White, *The Great Controversy*, pp. 611, 613.
[18] Article 15; see Stott, *Making Christ Known*, p. 49; section 24 in *Seventh-Day Adventists Believe*, pp. 333-346, "The Second Coming of Christ".
[19] This is the convincing argument of Russell Staples, "Adventism", in Donald W. Dayton and Robert K. Johnston (eds.), *The Variety of American Evangelicalism*, Knoxville: Univ. of Tennessee Press, 1991, pp. 57-71. Concerning the relationship between Adventists and evangelicals, see also Arthur F. Glasser, "A Friendly Outsider Looks at Seventh-day Adventists", *Ministry*, Vol. 62/1 (January 1989), pp. 8-10.

Eschatological Aspects: The Mission of the Near Advent and the Sabbath

In addition to its evangelical background and identity, Seventh-day Adventism has developed and continued to uphold some traits which stem from its Millerite and restorationist[20] roots and that give the church a particular sense of mission. The most outstanding of these characteristics are the belief in the imminent return of Jesus Christ and the observation of the Sabbath on Saturday.

The apocalyptic identity of Adventism has had a serious impact on its mission. While, in the early period, it hindered outreach because it made its believers to think that heaven is nearer than the unconverted, the belief in the soon return of Jesus has later provided a powerful incentive for many Adventists to dedicate themselves to evangelistic outreach or even cross-cultural mission service in order to warn people of the coming doom.[21] Although the idea that the proclamation of the gospel in the world had been accomplished already has been lingering in some parts of the church since its beginning up to the present, the commission to preach to all nations, tongues, and tribes *before* the end has become a major incentive for the world church to develop a new strategy to reach the whole globe. In spite of deviations such as renewed time-settings for the second advent and apocalyptic perfectionism on the fringe of Adventism, its awareness of biblical eschatology has helped the church not to fall into the trap of identifying itself fully with earthly activities while working to improve the temporal existence of both its members and the surrounding world.

While the hoped-for second coming of Jesus seemed to delay, the

---

[20] Pöhler, "Change in SDA Theology", p. 157-161, depicts restorationism/ primitivism, i.e. the idea that New Testament Christianity should be restored in the present time, as one of the most influential roots of SDA identity particularly because it was connected to millennialism that was so fundamental for the SDA experience. James White and Joseph Bates, the two major leaders of early sabbatarian Adventists, had been in restorationist groups before 1844.

[21] Cf. Andrews's statement about the purpose of his mission in Europe: "to preach the Sabbath, to warn the people of the coming judgment and to call God's people to obey the immutable law of God": John N. Andrews, "Meeting of Sabbathkeepers in Neuchâtel", RH, Vol. 25 (November 24, 1874), p. 172.

proclamation of Adventist Sabbath theology, in its roots being an element of restorationist thought, became the major eschatology-related missionary project of Adventism and actually *the* mark of Seventh-day Adventist identity even more than the somewhat less tangible "Blessed Hope". The Sabbath obtained an eschatological meaning among Adventists in that they believed it to be a crucial matter for the last days of history: Ellen White calls the Sabbath "the great test of loyalty", and traditionally, its observance has been equaled to the "seal of God" in Revelation 7:2 while Sunday keeping has been regarded as part of the eschatological "mark of the beast" (Revelation 13:17; 14:9), being a deviation from the divine law.[22] Furthermore, the messages of the 2nd and 3rd angels of Revelation 14 who announce the fallen state of Babylon and show an eschatological separation between worshippers of the "Beast" and those saints who "obey God's commandments and remain faithful to Jesus" are associated with the final conflict in which Seventh-day Adventists are believed to play a crucial double role: being both the true saints and the angels who bring the last warning to the world before the dreadful events of the end that usher the coming of Jesus.

Whereas eschatology seems not to have played a significant role in the mission of a number of other bodies for a considerable time, especially in the Catholic and mainline ("ecumenical") Protestant churches,[23] Adventism is a good example for David Bosch's thesis that "only in premillennial circles did the ... idea of a cataclysmic overthrow of the existing order survive, but ... premillennialists were completely marginalized".[24] Adventism seemed to exult in being ousted. They took this as a sign of being right and of the soon end, appealing, on the other hand, to those who, because of economical or social background, were also marginalized. This is probably the main reason why Adventist growth today occurs in the Two-Thirds World whereas most middle-class Whites do not find much attractive in traditional Adventism except they have been raised in a firmly Christian tradition.

Especially during the last two decades, some Adventist theologians,

---

[22] White, *Great Controversy*, pp. 604-605.
[23] Bosch, *Transforming Mission*, p. 501.
[24] *Ibid.*

mainly in the western world, have reinterpreted the focus of the church's eschatology. While maintaining doctrinal contents of the denomination's particular eschatological beliefs, the earlier focus on warning people of the imminent judgement has been changed to an emphasis on hope for today's man, this being a missionary attempt to reach out to the secular.[25] Still, others participated in the millennial fever of the year 2000 and propagated theories that attempted to prove that we live in the "very last days".[26]

Ecclesiological Aspects: The Missionary Remnant

A particular Seventh-day Adventist ecclesiology has been developed quite early in the history of the movement. The biblical terminology that Adventists have used frequently to describe its view of the true end-time church is that of the "Remnant".[27] This ecclesiological concept did not have an explicit missionary aspect in the beginning; rather, with reference to Revelation 12:17,[28] it emphasized the identity of Seventh-day Adventism with God's eschatological people who "keep His commandments" - including the Sabbath - and "hold to the testimony of Jesus", equated with the "Spirit of Prophecy" in Revelation 19:10 and believed to be present in the Seventh-day Adventist Church in the ministry of Ellen G. White.[29]

The Seventh-day Adventist movement connected the 3rd angel's

---

[25] See, e.g., Samuele Bacchiocchi, *The Advent Hope for Human Hopelessness: A Theological Study of the Meaning of the Second Advent for Today,* Berrien Springs: by the author, 1986; Fritz Guy, "The Future and the Present: The Meaning of the Advent Hope", in V. Norskov Olsen, *The Advent Hope in Scripture and History,* RHPA, 1987, pp. 211-229.

[26] G. Edward Reid, *Even at the Door,* by the author, 1994 [but, as his other book, *Sunday's Coming,* distributed by RHPA].

[27] "The Remnant and its Mission" is the 12th of the 27 Fundamental Doctrines held by the SDA Church; see *Seventh-Day Adventists Believe,* pp. 152-169 and appendix I of this study. Some OT verses referred to frequently in this context include 2 Chronicles 30:6; Ezra 9:14, 15; Isaiah 10:20-22; Jeremiah 42:2.

[28] "Those who obey God's commandments and hold to the testimony of Jesus" (NIV).

[29] *Seventh-Day Adventists Believe,* pp. 224-228.

message of Revelation 14:9-12 with the task of the Remnant whereas the 1st and 2nd angels' messages of Revelation 14:6-8 were seen to be fulfilled in the Millerite Movement. Thus, the Remnant began to be seen as an agency of both mission by example showing the world the character of God (Revelation 14:4) and messengers proclaiming a final warning to "Babylon" - the other churches[30] - because of its sins and perverted doctrines.

Over the decades, when the general gospel mission amongst non-Christians was included into Adventist Missiology, the concept of the Remnant, too, got a new aspect. One of today's leading missiologists in the church, Jon L. Dybdahl, argues that "the true purpose of this concept in the end is to broaden the scope of God's people. Even for Old Testament Israel, that broadening meant mission to the world."[31] Pointing to the recent mission experiences amongst Muslims, he asks whether the Remnant - and thus, Adventism - should not be seen as a reform movement among all world religions rather than merely out of other Christian churches.

A particular question has been, in the history of Adventism, how the Remnant and the Seventh-day Adventist Church relate to each other. Until present, there are voices who reaffirm the interpretation that the Seventh-day Adventist Church, as an organization, constitutes the Remnant church, and often stick to the expression "Remnant Church"[32] which is not found in the New Testament. However, especially since the 1950, there has been a tendency to view the denomination as a part of a larger Remnant,[33] leaving a tension[34] that also

---

[30] All the other churches were thought to have become, structurally and in teachings, Babylon when they rejected the Millerite Movement of the 1840s; Ellen White, *Early Writings*, RHPA, 1892, p. 279, calls them "doomed churches".
[31] Jon Dybdahl, "Mission Faces the 21st Century", in Baumgartner, *Re-Visioning Adventist Mission in Europe*, p. 56. The same argument is pursued by George R. Knight, "Remnant Theology and World Mission", in Dybdahl, *Adventist Mission in the 21st Century*, pp. 88-95.
[32] See, e.g., W.W. Fordham, "The Remnant Church", *Ministry*, Vol. 43 (June 1970), p. 61; Clifford Goldstein, *The Remnant*, PPPA, 1994.
[33] *Seventh-Day Adventists Answer Questions on Doctrine*, Washington, D.C.: Ministerial Association, General Conference of Seventh-day Adventists, pp. 177-202.

affects the mission of the church: the double role of Adventism as a denomination claiming superiority status and calling people to join it on one side and a movement bearing witness to people of different backgrounds is the challenge of the ecclesiological aspect of contemporary Adventist mission.

Somewhat contrarily to the "Babylon" view of other churches, there has been a high view of other Christians who work for winning souls to Christ in the denominational *Working Policy* since 1926, describing them as part of God's action in this world.[35] Thus, all other denominations are respected as being part of the Christian brotherhood and sisterhood.[36]

Another new approach to the identity of the church is reflected in a document about "Transitional Organizational Structures", recently accepted by the General Conference, and another document drafted by the Global Mission Issues Committee on "contextualized Adventist Communities". Against the traditional approach of incorporating every church resulting from missionary effort into the existing internationally uniform church structure, these documents allow new types of churches connected with the Seventh-day Adventist Church more loosely organizationally for the sake of missionary approaches that do not erect unnecessary structural barriers in unreached areas.[37] While the ideal of Organizational unity is maintained and should be sought according to these documents, the underlying theological concept is that the "Remnant" is not necessarily a visible organization although its main manifestation may be in it.

---

[34] These conflicting views both do have their own right, stressing the *ecclesia visibilis* and *ecclesia invisibilis* aspects of the church respectively.

[35] Section O 75 ("Relationships with Other Christian Churches and Religious Organizations") of the *General Conference Working Policy 1995-1996*, pp. 402; "Our Mission and Other Christians", unpublished Ms, Global Mission Working Group, 1996, p. 1.

[36] Ibid.

[37] "Transitional Organizational Structures", unpublished Ms, Global Mission Issues Committee, 1998; "Contextualized Adventist Communities", unpublished Ms, Global Mission Issues Committee, 1999.

Ellen G. White and the Seventh-day Adventist Missiological Perspective

Amongst early Seventh-day Adventists as well as during later periods, one of the most outstanding advocates and promoters of mission was Ellen G. White. Her identity as a prophetess helped her messages concerning the mission of the church to bear authority and urgency.[38]

As early as in 1848, it was her who, in spite of prevalent shut-door beliefs and the belief that the end was almost at hand, told her husband, James White, prophetic words that prompted him to start the mentioned first Seventh-day Adventist magazine in 1849:

> I have a message for you. You must begin to print a little paper and send it out to the people. Let it be small at first ... From this small beginning it was shown to me to be like streams of light that went clear round the world.[39]

In 1871, three years before Adventism sent out its first official missionaries, she had understood not only the need of missionary expansion but even the importance of human vessels as opposed to the earlier merely literature-based approach in mission as well as appropriate methodology:

> Young men should be qualifying themselves by becoming familiar with other languages...Our publications should be printed in other languages, that foreign nations may be reached. Much can be done through the medium of the press, but still more can be accomplished if the influence of the labors of the living preacher goes with our publications. Missionaries are needed to go to other nations to preach the truth in a guarded, careful manner.[40]

In the year of the first missionary's departure, she had already developed a missionary vision to reach the whole world:

> Our message is to go forth in power to all parts of the world - to Ore-

---

[38] In spite of opposition against this claim sometimes even inside the church not only in the early period but even after her death, e.g. by John Harvey Kellogg or Ludwig Richard Conradi; see Schwarz, *Light Bearers*, pp. 282-298, 475-476.
[39] Ellen White, *Life Sketches of Ellen G. White*, PPPA, 1915, p. 125.
[40] Ellen White, *Testimonies for the Church*, Vol. 3, PPPA, 1948, p. 204.

gon, to England, to Australia, to islands of the sea, to all nations, tongues and peoples.[41]

After these rather early statements about the world mission of the Seventh-day Adventist Church, Ellen White referred to this task more and more frequently, especially after having experienced mission situations herself in Europe and Australia.[42] Although the cultural differences she had to bridge in Australia were not as significant as for most of the missionaries in Europe and other countries, it was in these years of practical exposure to cross-cultural service that she got aware of the tasks involved in preparing and monitoring mission projects. She not only stressed the need of special missionary education as such,[43] she conceded also that in countries as India with their completely different cultural backgrounds, "the workers must go through a long course of education before the people can understand them, or they the people".[44] Being persuaded of the centrality of the task of mission in unreached lands, she ceaselessly called for gifts to be dedicated to missionary purposes.[45]

A unique contribution Ellen White made to Adventist Missiology at a time when anthropology and mission studies were still in their infancy were counsels concerning cultural issues that she gave both in particular situations and generally. Although the word "contextualization" did not yet exist, she made the concept behind it part of her message when she counselled in 1895 "that men should be wise in order that they may know how to adapt themselves to the peculiar ideas of the people" because "the people of every country have their own peculiar, distinctive characteristics".[46] Moreover, customs and climate should be considered when approaching people of other lands.[47]

In addition, her writings developed strategic missionary plans – e.g.,

---

[41] Ellen White, Ms 1, 1874.
[42] Ellen White, *Gospel Workers*, p. 465 [1888]; *Education*, PPPA, 1903, p. 262; *Life Sketches*, p. 338 [1892].
[43] White, *Life Sketches*, p. 374.
[44] Ellen White, *Testimonies for the Church*, Vol. 6, PPPA, 1948, p. 25.
[45] Ellen White, *Counsels on Stewardship*, RHPA, 1940, pp. 55, 133, 134; *Gospel Workers*, p. 467; *Testimonies*, Vol. 6, p. 27.
[46] Ellen White, *Testimonies to Ministers and Gospel Workers*, PPPA, 1923, p. 213.
[47] White, *Gospel Workers*, pp. 468-469.

using European immigrants to America to be sent back to Europe.[48] She advised not only to learn well the language of the people to be served, but also to understand cultural aspects of the Bible, thus calling for a kind of missionary hermeneutics of the Holy Scriptures.[49]

Ellen White's writings have continued to exercise great influence upon Missiology in the denomination. As in doctrinal and pastoral issues, Adventists have tended to seek support for a diversity of views from them, ranging from the call to leave the great cities in the endtime[50] – an anti-urban attitude that causes serious questions about the feasibility of urban mission – to radical readjustments in evangelistic methods. The various messages that the prophetess delivered in manifold different situations allows indeed several missiological conclusions depending on hermeneutic presuppositions and on how one sees the main role of the Seventh-day Adventist Church in the world today.

Most important, however, have been the voices of the leading Adventist missiologists[51] who quote Ellen White's statements concerning "varying circumstances taking place in our world that call for labor which will meet these peculiar developments"[52]. As Paul was "always shaping his message to the circumstances under which he was placed",[53] they infer that issues and challenges at stake today must be met with new approaches as described in the following section.

---

[48] White, *Testimonies*, Vol. 3, p. 205; Vol. 5, p. 392.
[49] White, *Counsels to Parents, Teachers, and Students*, PPPA, 1913, p. 518.
[50] The General Conference voted at its Annual Council of 1978 a document called *Country Living* emphasizing that Adventists should leave the great cities and do evangelism in it only from "outposts"; see Gottfried Oosterwal, "God Loves the Cities", in Richard Lehman et al., *Cast the Net on the Right Side*, p. 105. The idea did not materialize, however, to any considerable extent.
[51] E.g., Gottfried Oosterwal, former Director of the SDA Institute of World Mission, "The Process of Secularization", in Rasi and Guy, *Meeting the Secular Mind*, p. 61.
[52] Ellen White, Ms 8a, 1888.
[53] White, *Gospel Workers*, p. 300.

Chapter 3

Some Current Issues and Recent Developments

Secularism and Urbanization

A number of books on Adventist mission in the secular world have been published during the last 20 years, reflecting a growing awareness of missiological issues not only connected with the traditional "mission fields" but also with the "home base". These are both outstanding individual efforts[1] and collections of articles that have their origin in official church symposia and committees.[2] It is because of the process of an enlarging missionary vision in the denomination as a whole[3] that secularism as a "way of thought and life that is almost totally foreign to most Adventists"[4] was started to be explored by a group of Church leaders and researchers when General Conference president Neal C. Wilson called for a missionary emphasis on the secular world at the General Conference session in 1980.[5] It has become a fundamental insight for Adventism that the "(Unreached) People Group" concept of the Lausanne Movement should not only apply

---

[1] Jon Paulien, *Present Truth in the Real World: The Adventist Struggle to Keep and Share Faith in a Secular Society*, PPPA, 1993; Winfried Noack, *Gemeinde mit Zukunft*, AV, n.d. [ca. 1980].

[2] Baumgartner, *Re-Visioning Adventist Mission in Europe*; Lehmann et al., *Cast the Net on the Right Side*; Rasi and Guy, *Meeting the Secular Mind*.

[3] The General Conference Committee on Secularism even refers to secularism as the third great mission frontier for the SDA Church after Christianity and non-Christian religions; see "Report and Recommendations to the General Conference Committee", in Rasi and Guy, *Meeting the Secular Mind*, p. 187.

[4] William G. Johnsson, The Challenge of Secular Thought", in Rasi and Guy, *Meeting the Secular Mind*, pp. 14-15.

[5] Ibid.

to linguistic and ethnic units but also to sociological groups such as particular strata of secular society.[6]

Although dangerous elements have been recognized in secular world view and attitudes, especially the absence of a God who can be experienced as a reality as well as self-centeredness and competition as principles,[7] some SDA scholars have acknowledged that secular society has some positive sides which, if taken serious, can lead the church into a new phase of mission with opportunities for evangelism that have not been there before. Basic needs of secular people – fellowship and community as well as identity and an abundant, happy life – can be provided by the church more than by anything or anyone else.[8] Furthermore, Adventists know that the freedom of religion that secular societies provide is not only the very basis for the existence of a denomination like Seventh-day Adventism that does not support close co-operation with governments, but that it also frees people to being able to live a voluntary and thus a genuine faith.[9]

It is in the context of the encounter with the secular world, the city, and its institutions, that veteran missiologist Gottfried Oosterwal calls for "new Adventist lifestyles in technopolis, ... and greater involvement in the secular affairs and interests of society".[10] He demands that formerly mono-cultural and rurally oriented Adventist mission develop a new way of city Adventism. Instead of fleeing from the evils of the cities, Seventh-day Adventist mission "must also deal with the systems and structures of evil in the city, those systems that lead to

---

[6] "Report and Recommendations to the General Conference Committee", in Rasi and Guy, *Meeting the Secular Mind*, p. 191; Rolf J. Pöhler, "Religious Pluralism: A Challenge to the Contemporary Church", in Lehmann et al., *Cast the Net on the Right Side*, p. 83.

[7] J. Robert Spangler, "Secularization in New Testament Times", in Rasi and Guy, *Meeting the Secular Mind*, p. 117-124; "Report and Recommendations to the General Conference Committee", *ibid.*, p. 186.

[8] Gottfried Oosterwal, "The Process of Secularization", in Rasi and Guy, *Meeting the Secular Mind*, pp. 42-62.

[9] Ibid., pp. 47-48.

[10] Ibid., p. 60.

oppression, racism, injustice, corruption, neglect and idolatry".[11] Again, there is support from Ellen White's writings who at times urged people to settle in cities, open institutions, and participate in the affairs of the people in order to win them.[12]

One main fact that has been acknowledged in several of these studies dealing with secularism not only by leading Adventist scholars but also by administrators like the current Trans-European Division President, Bertil Wiklander, is that the Seventh-day Adventist Church must change its missionary strategies[13] which can imply changing theological emphasis: "The culture in which many of us grew up is no longer there! ... God does not change, but the way we see Him does."[14] Some have even come to the conclusion that talking about the "problem of secularism" is not correct and that the problem is in the church as much or even a lot more than in society. M. Pearson states in this context that in communication, problems in transmission are *always* the problem of the sender.[15]

This implies that in a sphere of pluralism, the traditional Adventist emphasis on accepting Bible teachings and making absolute claims about spiritual things must change to personal witness in order to be accepted by people; static dogmas that provided so much security to Adventists when society was still rather monolithic have to be modified to dynamic truths that make an impact on peoples' lives, and the church, while staying united in its basis theologically and organiza-

---

[11] Gottfried Oosterwal, "God Loves the Cities", in Lehmann et al., *Cast the Net on the Right Side*, p. 106.
[12] See the quotations ibid., 109 as well as Bruce Campbell Moyer, "God So Loves the City!", in Dybdahl, *Adventist Mission in the 21st Century*, pp. 206-212.
[13] "The churches have the medicine, but they fail to bring it to the receivers" (Bertil Wiklander, "The Secular Mind-Set and the Church - A Case Study", in Baumgartner, *Re-Visioning Adventist Mission in Europe*, p. 77).
[14] Bertil Wiklander, "It Needs to be Done", in Baumgartner, *Re-Visioning Adventist Mission in Europe*, p. 213.
[15] Michael Pearson, "The Problem of Secularism", in Lehmann et al., *Cast the Net on the Right Side*, pp. 90-101.

tionally, should become pluriform - a church where people of different backgrounds, emphases, and needs have a place.[16]

In this context, new concepts for the church in mission have been developed. "The Caring Church" concept developed by the General Conference in the early 1980s stresses the initiative of the "laity"[17] in local congregation as "headquarters" of the church and evangelism as a practiced adapted Adventist Christian lifestyle as opposed to mainly doctrine-centred proclamation and the tendency of clericalism.[18] Another interesting attempt on the theological level is to explore the meaning of some of the church's doctrines for secular people, e.g. the Sabbath as a God-given space of freedom from work-centred life in the modern world.[19]

Apart from dealing with secularism directly, it is mainly on the basis of the prevalent secularism in western societies that Adventist scholars have started to pay considerable attention to the Church Growth Movement and to incorporate many of its ideas into their publications and teaching.[20] Thus, Adventism, although it had started long ago to focus its attention not only on "foreign" mission but as much on "home" mission, has come into a phase in which the local church has come into its centre more than before.

---

[16] Rolf J. Pöhler, "Religious Pluralism", in Lehmann et al., *Cast the Net on the Right Side*, p. 87-88.

[17] Oosterwal frequently emphasizes the role of average church members and uses the term "laity" for them while rejecting its negative connotations of "non-professional" Christians.

[18] Gottfried Oosterwal, "The Process of Secularization", in Rasi and Guy, *Meeting the Secular Mind*, p. 60.

[19] Fritz Guy, "The Secular Meaning of the Sabbath", in Rasi and Guy, *Meeting the Secular Mind*, pp. 139-153; Reinder Bruinsma, *It's Time to Stop Rehearsing What we Believe and Start Looking at What Difference it Makes*, RHPA, 1997.

[20] See, e.g., Gottfried Oosterwal, *Patterns of SDA Church Growth in North America*, AUP, 1976; Erich Baumgartner's articles "The Church Growth Movement and the Value of Research" and "Megachurches and What They Teach Us", in Dybdahl, *Adventist Mission in the 21st Century*, pp. 132-142 and 150-158; George E. Knowles, *How to Help Your Church Grow*, RHPA, 1981; Roger L. Dudley, *Plant a Church, Reap a Harvest*. PPPA, 1989; *Handbuch für Gemeindeaufbau*. 3 vols. Darmstadt, Friedensau: Zentralstelle für Evangelisation und Gemeindeaufbau, 1993.

Mission among Muslims

Adventist mission among Muslims, as Christian Mission in general, has been quite unsuccessful in quantitative terms over many decades.[21] Islam, interpreted to be the fulfillment of the fifth trumpet of Revelation 9:1-12 by many Adventist interpreters of prophecy up to present,[22] was frequently seen as a satanic agency fighting against Christianity. Because of the general negative attitude against Islam coupled with the meagre promises of success in winning souls, Muslims rarely came into the focus of Adventism's missionary activities during most of its history.

On the other hand, since before World War II, there have been some individual attempts to reach Muslims in non-traditional ways. Wilhelm H. Lesovsky, a Czech-German SDA missionary in Lebanon from 1929 to 1939, not only suggested appreciation of and sympathy towards the Muslim way of life as a way of overcoming barriers between Muslims and Christians; he also developed the concept that there is a correspondence of Adventism with proto-Muslim belief. Therefore he demanded that Adventist mission become the princess of the missions in the midst of Islam and teach the others how to approach, thus forming a part of a world-wide movement to genuine faith.[23]

It was in the 1960s that a similarly positive approach towards Islam was further promoted by Robert C. Darnell who had come to the conclusion that Mohammed could be seen as a God-led reformer. He, too,

---

[21] Schantz, "Development of SDA Missionary Thought", p. 405, contended in the early 1980s that there were no former Muslims among the less than 3000 Seventh-day Adventists in the Middle East. This assertion is certainly too absolute.
[22] Robert J. Wieland, *The Revelation of Things to Come*, Rev. Ed., All Africa Publications, n.p., 1982, pp. 68-75.
[23] "Islam und Sabbathalter", unpublished Ms 1936, AEA, N 1-1, 168-200. This manuscript was to be considered at a General Conference session but seems not to have been discussed. For further studies on views on Islam in Adventism before World War II, see Thomas Vierus, "Das erkämpfte Bild vom Islam", Thesis, Darmstadt: Theologisches Seminar Marienhöhe, 1991; Stefan Höschele, "The Islam Conference 1935: Summing up Half a Century of Mission Experience", Term paper, Theologische Hochschule Friedensau, 1993.

emphasized the affinities between Seventh-day Adventists and Muslims - health laws and the emphasis on the judgement - and suggested to use Muslim terminology to bridge the gap between Muslims and Seventh-day Adventists. In spite of its innovative ways of reaching out to Muslims, there was, unfortunately, not much measurable outcome of the "Darnell School".[24] But since then, there has been a growing awareness of the need of serious study of Islam and new forms of encounter, reflected particularly in the establishment of the Seventh-day Adventist Global Centre for Islamic Studies in 1989 at Newbold College, England.[25]

It is quite recently that the idea of engaging in deep religious search together with Muslims has brought forth a breakthrough of Adventist mission in at least one southern Asian Islamic country. A movement of Muslims has been born who speak of themselves as "followers of Isa [= Jesus]" but remain culturally Muslims; some of them continue frequenting the mosque, and some observe other Islamic religious practices. While similar moves have been made by a larger number of Muslims,[26] a distinct group amongst these "Jesus Muslims" observes the Sabbath and considers itself as a part of the end-time "Remnant" that believes in Jesus as mediator and keeps God's commandments.[27] While this movement has been discussed not without controversies in

---

[24] Schantz, "Development of SDA Missionary Thought", pp. 405-410.

[25] This Center existed up to 1996 under the leadership of Borge Schantz when the Global Center for Adventist-Muslim Relations, based at the General Conference, its leader being Jerald Whitehouse, replaced its activities. Some of its publications were: Jonquil Hole and Borge Schantz (eds.), *The Three Angels and the Crescent: A Reader*, Bracknell: SDA Global Centre for Islamic Studies, 1993; Newsletter of the SDA Global Centre for Islamic Studies, Bracknell: 1989-1992; Adventist-Muslim Review, Bracknell: SDA Global Centre for Islamic Studies, 1993-1994; Borge F. Schantz, "Understanding Islam: Introduction to Islam and Muslim Evangelism", Photocopies of Transparencies, [Bracknell:] Global Centre for Islamic Studies, 1991; Borge Schantz, *Your Muslim Neighbour and You*, Bracknell: SDA Global Centre for Islamic Studies, 1993.

[26] Phil Parshall, "Danger! New Directions in Contextualization", *Evangelical Missions Quarterly*, Vol. 34/4 (October 1998), pp. 404-410.

[27] Jon Dybdahl, "Mission Faces the 21st Century", in Baumgartner, *Re-Visioning Adventist Mission in Europe*, p. 55, speaks of over 1500 individuals involved in this "Remnant" group in 1997.

the larger evangelical world, being labelled as syncretistic or close to that,[28] the existence of the mentioned group that is organizationally independent from the Seventh-day Adventist Church — though it resulted from Adventist missionary activities[29] — shows that this type of Mission amongst Muslims has become a major missiological issue for the denomination.

Jerald Whitehouse, Director of the Global Center of Adventist-Muslim Relations at the General Conference of Seventh-day Adventists and one of the major initiators of the movement, insists that spiritual growth is possible for Muslims.[30] He is one of the main Adventist advocates of establishing different kinds of congregations in Muslim contexts depending on the situation of the country and society, ranging, in a "contextualization continuum", from traditional Christian churches to secret believers, including groups with Christian faith but Islamic socio-religious identity.[31] This approach is complemented by a considerable number of other innovative scholars and missionaries amongst Muslims who have produced materials using mainly the Qur'an or other contextualized approaches.[32]

---

[28] One of the veterans in evangelical mission amongst Muslims, Phil Parshall, has recently strongly criticized the initiation of such movements; see his mentioned article "Danger! New Directions in Contextualization"; see also the following responses: Dean S. Gilliland, "Context is Critical in 'Islampur' Case", *Evangelical Missions Quarterly*, Vol. 34/4 (October 1998), pp. 415-417; John Travis [pseudonym], "Must all Muslims Leave 'Islam' to Follow Jesus?", *ibid.*, pp. 411-415.

[29] Jerald Whitehouse, "Adventist Christians, Cultural Muslims", *Spectrum*, Vol. 22/4 (October 1992), pp. 25-32.

[30] Personal conversation with Jerald Whitehouse, Mombasa, December 1997; [Jerald Whitehouse,] "Indicators for each of the Six Steps in Spiritual Growth, to Measure Progress", *Adventist-Muslim Relations Net Newsletter*, Vol. 1 (December 1996), p. 6.

[31] Jerald Whitehouse, "Muslim Peoples", in Baumgartner, *Re-Visioning Adventist Mission in Europe*, pp. 97-105; Jerald Whitehouse, "Contextual Adventist Mission to Islam: A Working Model", in *The Three Angels and the Crescent*, pp. 245-260; Jerald Whitehouse, "Reaching the Muslim World", in Dybdahl, *Adventist Mission in the 21st Century*, pp. 189-197.

[32] Abderrahim Al-Rumi [pseudonym], *The Qur'an is Right when it Says...*, Ostfildern: Die offene Tür, n.d.; Robert J. Wieland, *In Search of the Treasure of*

It has been recognized that the situation of Islam, similar to that of Judaism, is peculiar as compared to other religions in that there is no idol-worship nor any other practice clearly contrary to Christianity in official Islam that can be detected as an unbiblical element. Rather, the prophet Mohammed[33] brought monotheism to the polytheistic Arabs, giving them a status different from "pagans". Furthermore, the mentioned Muslim Jesus movement rejects Qur'anic interpretations that deny the death of Jesus and tries to interpret the Bible for a Muslim worldview, thus avoiding controversial doctrinal elements such as the Trinity. Here, Adventist missiologists can remind that several founders of the denomination, e.g., Uriah Smith and James White, held anti-Trinitarian beliefs up to the end of their lives.[34] It may be that the interaction with Islam can become an opening through which a new constructive relationship towards other religions will be possible.[35]

Theology of Religions and Ecumenism

Comparable experiments of adapted missionary methods have also been developed by Seventh-day Adventists in the context of Buddhism. Clifton Maberly, director of the Seventh-day Adventist Global Mission Study Center for Buddhism in Bangkok, Thailand, began in 1998 to lead a "contextualized Burmese Adventist Church service" in

---

Faith, All Africa Publications, n.d., no place indicated; Oscar Osindo, "Towards a Seventh-Day Adventist Mission to Muslims in Kenya", JATA, Vol. 2/1 (1996), pp. 92-104; Jonquil Hole and Borge Schantz (eds.), *The Three Angels and the Crescent*; Headley King [Pseudonym], "Tentmakers in the Arabian Gulf", *Spectrum*, Vol. 22/4 (October 1992), pp. 33-39; Borge Schantz, "Islam in Europe", in Lehmann et al., *Cast the Net on the Right Side*, pp. 55-68; Sampson K. Twumasi, "The Challenge of Folk Islam in East Africa", JATA, Vol. 3/1 (November 1997), pp. 92-99.

[33] Hugh I. Dunton, "Prophets in Parallel: Mohammed and Ellen G. White - Adventism and Islam Share a Respect for the Prophetic Gift", *Spectrum*, Vol. 22/4 (October 1992), pp. 40-51.

[34] Pöhler, "Change in SDA Theology", pp. 168-173.

[35] There have even been individual SDA missionaries' attempts of participating in Muslim prayer or praying together with Muslims; see, e.g., Marcel Pichot, "The Village of Bendougou", *Adventist Frontiers* 15/4 (April 1999), p. 21.

Yangon, Myanmar, in addition to projects such as "Psalm 23 mantra sheets" being distributed and a "meditation house" being built in Burma as well as Burmese gospel paintings that are designed to explain the Christian gospel for Buddhists.[36] The results of these ventures still have to be awaited. Surprisingly, amongst the church's missiologists and international leaders, there seems to have been little opposition against these far-reaching attempts of contextualization. This leads to the question of a Seventh-day Adventist Theology of Religions.

Once, when Seventh-day Adventism was an inner-Christian reform movement, the theological assessment of religions outside Christianity had not been a major issue. The Catholic Church and the Protestant churches were a world that seemed to be sufficient for early Adventism. It was they who were seen as the end-time context of persecution and as main actors in the drama of the book of Revelation, the Beast and its image.[37] The world outside North America and Europe was absent in Adventist eschatology and Missiology.

On the other hand, Ellen White suggested in several instances that the heathen can be saved, even if though not through their religion, but at least instead of it. As early as 1871, she stated that "angels of God are moving on the hearts and consciences of the people of other nations",[38] implying that God prepares those who have either not heard the Adventist message or the Christian gospel at all. Clearer, the possibility of salvation is stated in 1917: "scattered in every land, there are those who have not bowed the knee to Baal";[39] even heathen sacrifices are seen to be an avenue through which Babylonian pagans became interested in the Hebrew worship and the Redeemer.[40] Seventh-day Adventist Missiology, being developed later than Seventh-

---

[36] Jonathan Gallagher, "First ever Contextualized Burmese Adventist Church Service", Adventist News Network, February 24, 1998; Personal conversation with Clifton Maberly, Mombasa, December 1997; Clifton Maberly, "Buddhism and Adventism: A Myanmar Initiative", in Dybdahl, *Adventist Mission in the 21st Century*, pp. 232-240.
[37] White, *Great Controversy*, pp. 563-592; cf. Revelation 13.
[38] White, *Testimonies*, Vol. 3, p. 202.
[39] Ellen White, *Prophets and Kings*, PPPA, 1917, p. 188.
[40] Ellen White, *The Desire of Ages*, PPPA, 1898, p. 28.

day Adventist eschatology, seems to provide ingredients lacking in early, eschatology-focused denominational theology.

The necessity of relating to other religions in a meaningful way was recently recognized more than before by Adventists and is reflected in one project associated with the Global Mission Initiative: Seventh-day Adventist Religious Study Centres. Since the late 1980s, the General Conference has been establishing centres for the study of Hinduism, Buddhism, Islam, and Jewish Religion. They have been commissioned to explore Adventism's relation with these religions and to come up with ways to reach their adherents with the Gospel. During the last few years, the directors of these centres have been dealing with issues arising from the encounter with other religions, such as the use of sacred writings of other religions, church organization in non-Christian areas, etc., providing a ferment that not only allows but demands the development of new missionary models and methods.[41]

One attempt of evaluating a non-Christian religion with a relationship to Adventism appeared in *Saturday God and Adventism in Ghana*.[42] Here, Owusu-Mensa, a Ghanaian, displays a positive attitude towards the traditional religion of the Akan of Ghana who worshipped the High God *Onyamee Kwaame* ("Saturday God"). Although Owusu-Mensa does not explore much the meaning of this traditional religion for Seventh-day Adventism[43] and admits that the Saturday God background did not help Adventist mission much[44] - partially because other mission societies entered Ghana before - the study is a good example of an unbiased and constructive Seventh-day Adventist approach to religions outside Christianity. A similar, but much shorter study has

---

[41] See the following unpublished Mss: Global Mission Issues Committee, "Contextualization and SDA Mission", 1998; "Contextualized Adventist Communities", 1999; "Fundamental Beliefs and Preparation for Baptism", 1999; "The Use of Non-Christian Writings in Mission", 1998; "Transitional Organizational Structures", 1998.

[42] Kofi Owusu-Mensa, *Saturday God and Adventism in Ghana*, Frankfurt: Lang, 1993.

[43] This book is rather descriptive; actually, it consists of two separate units, one dealing with traditional Akan religion and one with the history of Adventism in Ghana.

[44] *Ibid.*, pp. 72-73.

been recently published by Sammy N'Getich concerning the Kalenjin of Kenya who seem to have had practices related to the biblical Sabbath.[45]

A recent contribution on the Theology of Religions argues that Adventist theology and mission is "neither inclusivist, exclusivist or pluralistic" concerning the question to which extent Jesus Christ is the only way of salvation; rather, it emphatically states that Adventists do believe that there is salvation through Jesus Christ, and this is the reason for mission. The merit this view has is that theories about issues not clearly outlined in the Holy Scriptures may divide while the call to mission is a unifying factor that Adventists share.[46]

Surprisingly, the issue of ecumenism - initially an agenda of churches co-operating in mission - seems to have been a much more difficult chapter of Seventh-day Adventist theology and Missiology than the relation to other religions. There have not been many Adventist statements and publications that speak positively about adherents of other Christian denominations.[47] For a long time, the main problem between Adventism and other denominations was that, while other churches called Adventism a "sect", the denominational eschatology attributed to them the identity of being a part of the eschatological "Babylon".

This theological persuasion found its missionary application in converting people out of other churches. It has not only been applied to the denominations present when the Seventh-day Adventist Church

---

[45] "Sabbath-Keeping Traditions in Africa: The Case of the Kalenjin People of Kenya", JATA, Vol 2/1 (November 1996), pp. 45-53.

[46] Derek C. Beardsell, "The Unfinished Task: Is there Salvation outside Christianity? Do other Christian Churches also Fulfill the Great Commission?", in Dunton et al., *Adventist Missions Facing the 21st Century*, pp. 25-37. Beardsell does not attempt to answer or even treat the second question in his essay but the title shows that it belongs to the first.

[47] See, e.g., Morris Venden [SDA Evangelist], *What I like about...* [Lutherans, Baptists, Methodists, Charismatics, Catholics, Jews, Adventists], PPPA, 1986; Jacob J. Nortey, "Sabbath (7th Day)-Keeping African Independent Churches and the Seventh-Day Adventists in Ghana", in Dunton et al., *Adventist Missions Facing the 21st Century*, pp. 180-192; Wolde-Endreas, Solomon, "The Abyssinian Church: History and Missiology, *ibid.*, pp. 164-179.

was born. Adventism has also been very critical in view of the growth of Pentecostalism and the Charismatic movement. The belief prevails in many Adventist circles that these currents constitute a false awakening that heralds the soon end of the world.[48] Thus, it is only in few areas that Adventism has been touched by Charismatic, and it has usually brought great conflict, not the missionary renewal that other groups have experienced. Only a minority of Adventist leaders have seen the charismatic revival as a positive force[49] although miraculous signs, healings, and related phenomena are accepted by Adventists as God's work.[50]

One of the main reasons for the Seventh-day Adventist Church not to join the World Council of Churches is a missiological question - the question of "proselytism". Originally, the meaning of this word – that later became a label frequently assigned to those who do not conform with ecumenical ideas of evangelization – was propaganda which used means that were illegitimate: material promises, psychological pressure, or misusing ignorance, for "soul-snatching" purposes - practices that Adventists do not agree with, too.[51] This concept, however, has been substituted by the notion that member churches of the WCC should not try to win over nor accept the conversion of members of other churches participating in the WCC. This is unacceptable for the denomination and does, according to its view, directly oppose one of the most basic rights of religious liberty, the right to change religious

---

[48] Some of the SDA publications that portray such a critical view are: Gerhard F. Hasel, *Speaking in Tongues: Biblical Speaking in Tongues and Contemporary Glossolalia*, Berrien Springs: Adventist Theological Society Publications, 1991; Rene Noorbergen, *Charisma of the Spirit - in Search of a Supernatural Experience: A Journalist Looks at the Tongues Movement*, PPPA, 1973; a more balanced views is presented in William E. Richardson, *Speaking in Tongues: Is it still the Gift of the Spirit?*, RHPA, 1994.
[49] See, e.g., Winfried Noack, "Teachings of the World-Wide Revival", in Lehmann et al., *Cast the Net on the Right Side*, pp. 117-132.
[50] See, e.g., Pardon Mwansa, "Healings and Miraculous Signs in World Mission", in Dybdahl, *Adventist Mission in the 21st Century*, pp. 125-131.
[51] Although some Adventists may have used some of these practices (especially psychological pressurizing), they are against SDA principles; furthermore, similar elements can be found in almost every religious organization.

affiliation.[52] The *General Conference Working Policy* stipulates:

> The Seventh-day Adventist Church is unable to confine its mission to restricted geographical areas because of its understanding of the gospel commission's mandate. ... In the origin and rise of the Seventh-day Adventist people, the burden was laid upon us to emphasize the gospel of Christ's second coming as an imminent event, calling for the proclamation of Biblical truths in the setting of the special message of preparation as described in Bible prophecy, particularly in Revelation 14:6-14."[53]

The Seventh-day Adventist Church also believes, while respecting the WCC, that the hope that churches, when united in mission, will be more effective, has actually failed. For Seventh-day Adventists, it is an illusion that a movement that works for unity on the basis of minimum agreements can help the church spread the gospel including everything that Jesus Christ has commissioned to His Church. History indeed seems to show that as far as the evangelistic and cross-cultural missionary dimensions are concerned, WCC member churches have continuously decreased their activities.[54]

On the other hand, Adventism has not been reluctant to be an observer in the WCC and related organizations, e.g. on national level ecumenical associations, and to dialogue with representatives of ecumenical bodies and other churches, this being part of its mission.[55] For this and related purposes, the church has established an Advisory Council that can organize dialogues and meetings.[56] It has usually presented its identity primarily as being part of the family of Protes-

---

[52] Bert Beverly Beach, ... *auf daß sie alle eins seien*, Ed. by Gemeinschaft der Siebenten-Tags-Adventisten [in der DDR = SDA in the GDR], Berlin: Union Verlag, 1977, pp. 104-109; Bert B. Beach, "Ecumenism and Evangelization", in Lehmann et al., *Cast the Net on the Right Side*, pp. 28-29.

[53] Section O 75 ("Relationships with Other Christian Churches and Religious Organizations") of the *General Conference Working Policy 1995-1996*, pp. 402.

[54] Bert Beverly Beach, ... *auf daß sie alle eins seien*, pp. 91-102.

[55] "World Council of Churches/Seventh-Day Adventist Conversation", *Ecumenical Review*, Vol. 24/2 (April 1972), pp. 9-23;

[56] "Stellungnahme der Generalkonferenz hinsichtlich der Beziehungen zu anderen Religionsgemeinschaften", *Aller Diener* (3+4/1984), p. 61.

tantism, emphasizing its common heritage with other denominations,[57] calling them brothers and sisters, and seeking opportunities of fellowship and shared spiritual experience.[58]

Public Issues, Politics, and Poverty

If one agrees that the mission of the church, while focusing on evangelism as central task, does not exclude other lines of service to humankind, an Adventist Missiology also has to tackle manifold issues of society that concern the church. Although SDA missiologist Borge Schantz has contended that "areas of mission obligation that are almost completely neglected by Seventh-day Adventists are the complex matter of social responsibility",[59] it is not true that Adventism has been too slow to develop activities pertaining to public life and social service. It has been part of its mission philosophy from the beginning to serve holistically, aiming at restoring the dignity of man in its social, physical, mental, and spiritual aspects.[60] Thus, in spite of putting much weight on their spiritual mission, Adventists have not failed to serve people in aspects of life that are not primarily religious.

For more than 100 years, the church has been active in the field of religious liberty. Initially founded because of conflicts with the US government about Sunday laws in various US states, the SDA-sponsored journal *Liberty*[61] together with the *International Religious Liberty Association* (USA) have expanded their focus on religious liberty World-Wide. A similar work is done by its European counterpart, the *Internationale Vereinigung zur Verteidigung und Förderung der Religionsfreiheit* (Switzerland) with its journal *Conscience and Lib-*

---

[57] See, e.g., W. Mueller, *Der Dienst der Mission*: Mueller describes Adventism as one of the Protestant Missions and quotes Gustav Warneck and other mission scholars to support the general idea of mission in other countries, thus presenting not SDA specific but general mission apologetics.
[58] "Our Mission and Other Christians", unpublished Ms, Global Mission Working Group, 1996.
[59] Schantz, "Development of SDA Missionary Thought", p. 743.
[60] Cf. W. Mueller who refers, in his apologetic work *Der Dienst der Mission*, to all of these aspects of SDA mission.
[61] *Fides et Libertas*, published by the same organization, has been started in 1998.

erty. Both associations have been instrumental in bringing together renowned scholars and representatives of diverse religious and political backgrounds[62] at various congresses and in promoting religious liberty at the world/UN, European Council, and national levels.[63] There are few other organizations that have been active to a similar degree in this field.

An even more intrinsic part of Adventist mission to society is its particular emphasis on healthful living or a "health reform" that has frequently been called "the right arm of the Three Angels' Messages" according to a statement by Ellen White.[64] Apart from building famous medical institutions such as Loma Linda University and the early 20th century magnet of natural medicine, Battle Creek Sanitarium, as well as many Adventist hospitals in the Two-Thirds World being leading in quality in their respective country, Adventists have distinguished themselves from other denominations by integrating the health aspect into their doctrine and lifestyle. An Adventist is supposed to abstain from alcohol and smoking as well as from unhealthy food of all kinds, including meat that is unclean according to Leviticus 11. The promotion of restoring human beings not only spiritually but also physically is a central idea of the church's mission to the world.[65]

In spite of traditional reservations about Seventh-day Adventist participation in politics, the growing membership in both Western countries and the Two-Thirds World has brought forth the existence of Adventist politicians in many lands. In some areas this is almost inevitable because, different from the humble beginnings in 19th century North America, Adventists today constitute a majority or even almost

---

[62] Using two randomly chosen issues of *Conscience and Liberty*, Vol. 19 No. 36 and, Vol. 20 No. 38, they show that renowned scholars like Mohammed Arkoun and Muhammad Hamidullah have written articles for *Conscience and Liberty*, and at congresses, Daniel arap Moi and John S. Pobee have spoken. Léopold Senghor is president of the Honorary Committee of Conscience and Liberty.

[63] The European association is recognized by the European Council and the UN and UNESCO with advisory status; see *Conscience and Liberty* cover inside.

[64] White, *Testimonies*, Vol. 6, pp. 229, 327.

[65] See article 20 (Christian Behavior) in *Seventh-Day Adventists Believe*, pp. 278-292 as well as the SDA Mission Statement in Appendix I.

all of the population in some areas.[66] In other cases Adventist politicians have been instrumental in the reconstruction and development of younger countries.[67]

Perhaps the most famous Seventh-day Adventist contribution to society lies in its various types of institutions - medical, educational, publishing, etc. - some of which can be found in most countries of the world today. It is very important to ask why Adventism, originally an apocalyptic movement waiting for the imminent end of the world, has succeeded to develop, e.g., the most comprehensive Protestant educational system. This has led to the outsider observation: "Seldom while expecting a Kingdom of God from heaven has a group worked so diligently for one on earth".[68] The answer lies not simply in the fact that Adventists were American pragmatists; rather, the very eschatological vision was translated into missionary activity by Adventists when they became clear about the fact that they could "not know the day or the hour"[69] of Jesus' return who was actually waiting for them to do their part for Him to come. Thus, Ellen White said:

> Let no one conclude that, because the end is near, there is no need of special effort to build up the various institutions as the cause shall demand. You are not to know the day or the hour of the Lord's appearing ... Since the Lord is soon coming, it is time to put out our money to the exchangers, time to put every dollar we can spare into the Lord's treasury, that institutions may be established for the education of workers.[70]

In the field of social service, it can be acknowledged that, especially during the post-World War II years, the Seventh-day Adventist Church has been tirelessly engaged in new ventures of mission.

---

[66] E.g., in Kisii, south west Kenya, or in a part of South Pare, Tanzania.
[67] See, e.g., the somewhat hagiographic popular book of Delbert W. Baker, *From Exile to Prime Minister: How Samson Kisekka, a Christian Physician, is Successfully Leading Uganda from Ruin to Restoration*, RHPA, 1988.
[68] Winthrop Hudson [former president of the American Society of Church History] in *Religion in America*, New York: Charles Scribner's Sons, 1965, p. 347; quoted in Roy Branson, "Adventists Between the Times: The Shift in the Church's Eschatology", *Spectrum*, Vol. 8/1 (September 1976), p. 13.
[69] Matthew 25:13 (NIV).
[70] White, *Testimonies*, Vol. 6, pp. 440-441 [published originally in 1900].

Adventist Development and Relief Agency (ADRA), founded in 1956 as Seventh-day Adventist Welfare Service, Inc. (SAWS), expanded significantly through the decades[71] and was reorganized in 1983 under the present name to put more emphasis on development than on "aid" or relief in cases of catastrophes.[72] ADRA is today one of the few agencies still working in Somalia; and in the early 90s in the war around Sarajevo, former Yugoslavia, it was also almost the only organization still getting into the town. There are today academic departments of development studies, e.g. at Andrews University, one of the leading Adventist universities, and at Friedensau, the SDA college in Germany.

While especially ADRA's relief work in humanitarian catastrophes has been outstanding, Adventism's attitude towards development service/development co-operation must still be studied more. Perhaps the most important issue in Adventism's development work for this study is the question how the church relates its eschatology and Missiology to these activities. SDA policies concerning ADRA which contain a special section on the biblical-theological foundations of its work do not only state that God has a special concern for the poor and that following Jesus and the principle of love means that the Church should provide a holistic healing ministry to the people of the world without considering their religious, racial, or political background. Christianity is even called a "catalyst in social and political change", but the Church, as an organization, should "not seek political involvement".[73] Most interesting because specifically Adventist is section 6:

> The end time brings cruel and evil distortions in the social fabric, a condition deplored in the world and by its Lord, and to which the church responds. (James 5:1-6; Isa 58:6,7, Rev 3:17)[74]

---

[71] John, Harrison W., "SAWS expands Its Focus", *Spectrum*, Vol. 12/3 (April 1982), pp. 15-21.
[72] "Commissioned to Serve: Adventist Development and Relief Agency", Silver Spring: ADRA, n.d. [Brochure published for the 1995 SDA GC session], p. 1.
[73] Section HA 15 ("Basis for Supporting Philosophy for ADRA") in the *General Conference Working Policy 1995-1996*, p. 312.
[74] *Ibid.*

Here, an eschatological Missiology of social responsibility finds a basis by applying the self-image of Adventism as church of the last days to the realities of the world in the time that Adventism believes to exist for. It is stated further that the church does have a concern especially for the very poor and all kinds of victims of human need, but that not only emergency needs should be cared for but that providing long-term solutions is essential,[75] proving that eschatological orientation does not need to result in short-sightedness but can be a ferment that looks at the world realistically.[76]

In concluding this section, one can say that Adventism has come to a point where a broad range of missionary concepts and activities are included in its Missiology.

Cultural Issues and Contextualization

Especially during the last one or two decades, the issue of cultural diversity has become a major issue in the international Seventh-day Adventist Church not only as a practical problem but also as a theological and missiological issue. One recent example: After much discussion and various publications concerning the matter, the 1990 and 1995 General Conference sessions voted not to allow the ordination of women pastors to the gospel ministry in the world and in individual Divisions, respectively. This decision reflects the fact that the cultural realities of a world church are quite diverse and that it is not easy to deal with cultural differences especially because they are often presented as theological differences.

Indeed, it seems that there are incompatible underlying theological emphases in today's Seventh-day Adventist Church that necessarily lead to conclusions opposing each other in practical as well as missiological matters. Van Wyk has called one Adventist theological

---

[75] *Ibid.*, pp. 307-308.
[76] A few more historical and theological considerations on the work of ADRA are found in David R. Syme, "Crossing Boundaries – ADRA and AWR", in Dybdahl, *Adventist Mission in the 21st Century*, pp. 198-205.

approach the "confessional school"[77] which is not ready to contextualize traditional Seventh-day Adventist beliefs to any considerable extent, even concerning elements that are not central as lifestyle questions such as adornment or dress. On the other side, there are critics if traditionalism: some observe that Adventism, in some countries, tends to be very strongly dominated by American cultural patterns, and call for a cultural identity change. Others like van Wyk who can be labelled "progressive Adventists" believe that Adventism is not an immutable monolithic block but rather has the tradition of progressive adaptation of diverse ideas and practices that fit into its main thrust of being an eschatological-restorationist movement.[78]

Contextualization has become an important issue in the denomination because it addresses both hermeneutics and mission which are two major concerns particularly since the 1980s in the Seventh-day Adventist Church.[79] A crucial document recently passed by the General Conference has called contextualization "a part of the mission of the Seventh-day Adventist Church",[80] indicating that there is a concern in missiological thinking that Adventism become truly a church for all nations, tribes, tongues, and peoples. According to this document, while Adventist contextualization is "to uphold the 27 fundamental beliefs", local expressions of Adventism should be encouraged. Wiklander, in a related discussion paper, stresses that contextualization has the purpose of salvation[81] - and, I conclude, is thus a missionary activity. The new awareness about the necessity of contextualization has also led to the far-reaching conclusion that documents such as the 27 Beliefs, the *Church Manual*, and the Baptismal Vows "were

---

[77] Gerhard van Wyk, "A Perspective Approach to Contextualization", JATA, Vol. 3/1 (November 1995), pp. 29-44; Gerhard van Wyk, "A Practical Theological Perspective on Adventist Theology and Contextualisation", JATA, Vol. 1/1 (November 1995), pp. 132-149.
[78] Ibid.
[79] The heat of the hermeneutical discussion among Adventists is well reflected in Samuel Koranteng-Pipim, *Receiving the Word: How New Approaches to the Bible Impact Our Biblical Faith and Lifestyle*, Berrien Springs: Berean, 1996.
[80] "Contextualization and SDA Mission", unpublished Ms, Global Mission Issues Committee, 1998.
[81] Bertil Wiklander, "The Boundaries of Contextualisation in Mission", pp. 7-8.

framed in the context of a relationship to other Christians. The mission to non-Christians demands that we understand and relate to these statements in new ways."[82]

One example from the field of Adventism confronting cultural issues that shall illustrate the question of contextualization is the question of polygamy. When Adventists entered areas where polygamy was an accepted form of marriage, the church first responded by condemning the custom and by reaffirming monogamy as the only valid mode of marriage for Seventh-day Adventists or those who wanted to be baptized.[83] During the period between 1931 and 1941, however, the church decided to grant freedom to those fields that faced this problem to decide on their own whether or not to accept certain polygamous baptismal candidates for baptism and a "probationary" membership.[84] Subsequently, this action was again reversed, and from then on, polygamists had to divorce all their wives except one in order to be eligible for baptism.[85]

In the 1970s and 80s, the General Conference set up a study group to reconsider the issue which recommended a slightly revised policy in favour of accepting polygamists under certain circumstances. This recommendation, though, was never voted. Thus, in spite of several important voices advocating change because of the rather western than biblical background of rigidly prohibiting polygamy,[86] contextualization did not reach very far in this case. At least, the discussion has been attempted.[87]

---

[82] "Fundamental Beliefs and Preparation for Baptism", unpublished Ms, Global Mission Issues Committee, 1999.

[83] Russell Staples, "The Church and Polygamy in Sub-Saharan Africa", unpublished Ms, 1981, p. 43.

[84] Ibid., p. 44.

[85] Ibid., p. 45; *General Conference Working Policy 1995-1996*, p. 90f (section C 85).

[86] William G. Johnsson, "Between the Ideal and the Actual", AR 163/22 (May 29, 1986), pp. 4-5.

[87] Recently, there has been an SDA study that claims that polygamy can not be justified biblically under any circumstances: Ronald A.G. DuPreez, "Polygamy in the Bible with Implications for Seventh-Day Adventist Missiology", DMin, AU, 1993.

More recent events have clearly shown that cultural uniformity is not a reality any more in Adventist churches of different countries. The 1998 World-Wide satellite evangelism or its 1999 and 2000 Africa-wide counterparts was brought into most towns of the Christian world; and Adventists found, at times with some degree of shock, that there is unity in theology to a large extent but great diversity in cultural practices, including the use of music, dancing, jewellery, and attire.[88] Adventists have to ask themselves how much they want to be a counter-culture,[89] how much they want to honour their American heritage and in which areas they want to adapt to local circumstances.[90] If the Adventist church wants to be a church for all nations, it must both maintain a clear identity *and* encourage its members to take cultural roots in different contexts, producing *African* Adventism, *Indian* Adventism, etc.

---

[88] Many Tanzanian Adventists, e.g., were surprised to see the way American or West African Adventists dress, sing, and (as they perceived it in some musical performances) "dance".

[89] Cf. lifestyle questions like rejecting the use of alcohol, tobacco, and meat considered unclean according to Leviticus 11, but also traditionally strongly emphasized prohibitions like jewellery and dress codes.

[90] E.g., most of the Kisii, South West Kenya, live from planting tea, an activity traditionally rejected by Adventists because of the negative health implications of tea; many of the Kisii Adventists also do drink tea, a practice rejected amongst Adventists in the USA.

Chapter 4

Final Remarks: The Future of Seventh-Day Adventist Missiology

As a strongly future-oriented religious movement, Adventism has to reflect missiologically on its development in the time to come - as a part of its present mission. The "signs of the times" and "present truth", dynamic concepts that lie at the very heart of Adventism, have to be considered when analyzing the task that lies ahead for this church. As mission and Missiology have always been inseparably connected with the Seventh-day Adventist Church as a whole, I suggest that the following issues facing the denomination are the most important missiological fields of the future to be reflected upon in addition to the issues discussed in the previous chapter:

Growth Explosion or Slowing Down? Expansion and its Consequences

At present, one can see a great variety of growth patterns in different parts of the Seventh-day Adventist Church. Annual growth ranges from below 0% in some parts of Europe to 15% and above in various African countries. The question, however, is how long this staggering growth in some areas of he Two-Thirds World will continue and when a slowing down process is to be expected - in one or two decades? This leads to an increased importance of responding to the challenge of re-thinking missionary strategies as it is reflected in the *Global Mission* initiative and other cross-cultural missionary movements and organizations. Furthermore, experiences like the doubling of church membership in Russia after the fall of Communism in a few years and the subsequent loss of almost half of the new members converted in public evangelistic meetings have to be addressed and evaluated.[1]

Another missiological challenge arising from the success in growth is the question of how Adventism can function where the reality of a folk church (i.e., majority church) has changed the "remnant" paradigm, especially in several African countries where whole tribes or regions have become Adventist. Sociologically speaking, the way "sect" and "church" structures relate to each other in Adventism is a huge challenge for the denomination but has hardly been addressed yet by missiologists.[2] Related to this, particularly in those countries where Adventists are a significant force in society, is the general question of how they should relate to political and social movements and questions. There are cases like the Rwanda catastrophe of 1994 where Adventism, though being an important force in society, seems not to have played any significantly positive role.

Administration: Uniformity, Disintegration, or Pluriformity?

Up to the present, some Adventists boast that theirs is the most widespread Protestant denomination. Whether this is true or not, the Organizational unity that has made it to be such an international and still unified movement is part of its self-understanding as the "Remnant". However, the rather uniform pattern of administrative units World-Wide may one day break up or will have to give way to a more pluriform organization. Calls for change have been voiced for many years, pointing to the fact that the existing church structure was estab-

---

[1] For one attempt in this context, see Bill Knott, "With all Deliberate Speed: A Study of Pace in Mission", *Spectrum*, Vol. 12/3 (April 1982), pp. 11-14.

[2] The topic has been addressed, however, by the Adventist sociologist of religions, Ronald Lawson, in his articles "Broadening the Boundaries of Church-Sect Theory: Insights from the Evolution of the Non-Schismatic Mission Churches of Seventh-Day Adventism", *Journal for the Scientific Study of Religion*, Vol. 37/4 (September 1998), pp. 652-672, and "Sect-State Relations: Accounting for the Differing Trajectories of Seventh-day Adventists and Jehovah's Witnesses", *Sociology of Religion*, Vol. 56/4 (1995), pp. 351-377.

lished when it had hardly 100,000 members.³ As in the 1901 reorganization, the mission of the church has to be re-translated into viable structures; the difference is that this probably has to be done in different ways world-wide according to local needs. Two recent official documents about "Transitional Organizational structures" and "Contextualized Adventist communities" have highlighted the need of missiological consideration of church administration.⁴

Another aspect of particular importance in the field of administration is the question of finance.⁵ As a world church, there has been a traditionally strong North American dominance in both funding and decision-making connected with finance. Models will have to be developed that enable the different world fields to co-operate in a truly missionary partnership.⁶

Theology: Fundamentalism, Loss of Identity, or Missionary Theology?

The last area of missiological interest is the area that has unified Adventism traditionally most: its theology. At present, one can observe several theological tendencies in the Seventh-day Adventist Church apart from a "mainline" Adventism that is probably the cur-

---

³ See *Spectrum*, Vol. 14/4 (March 1984) with its articles of James W. Walters, "The Need for Structural Change", pp. 14-18, "A Call for an Open Church", pp. 18-24, "Defining Participation: A Model Conference Constitution", pp. 25-35, and Raymond F. Cottrell, "The Varieties of Church Structure", pp. 40-53.

⁴ "Transitional Organizational Structures", unpublished Ms, Global Mission Issues Committee, 1998; "Contextualized Adventist Communities", unpublished Ms, Global Mission Issues Committee, 1999.

⁵ This issue has been referred to by Borge Schantz in articles which partially overlap: "Seventh-day Adventist Missionary Finance: Is Reform Needed?", in Dybdahl, *Adventist Mission in the 21st Century*, pp. 96-104, and "Towards a Theology of Seventh-day Adventist Mission Finance", Dunton et al., *Adventist Missions Facing the 21st Century*, pp. 124-138.

⁶ One such new model of more international co-operation is the plan recently adopted by the world church to share the expenses of the General Conference, including operating expenses and appropriations to Divisions, on a more equal basis than before, although North America will still contribute 6% of its budget while other Divisions will contribute 2%; see Ray Dabrowski, "New Formula for Financing Adventist Church Mission Voted", ANN (25 April 2000).

rent that still has the strongest influence: "evangelical" Adventism that emphasizes the centrality of the cross and tends to downplay the traditional Adventist emphasis on the law; "historical" Adventism, the traditionalist wing that insists on the Seventh-day Adventist "pillars" as most important aspects of denominational identity, and "progressive" Adventism that tries to dialogue with people of the modern world and make Adventism as relevant as possible for the present.[7]

Whatever theological currents one may favour: if the Seventh-day Adventist Church continues to stress its unique theological tenets while being in constant and close contact with the various worlds around it, I believe that it can avoid the dangers of both narrow fundamentalism and loss of identity. Rather, it will continue to work out a missionary theology that seeks to communicate in manifold ways the "everlasting gospel to all nations".[8] This is not yet a reality everywhere, but it remains a missionary task for Adventism – a task that will never end until Jesus Christ comes and the Kingdom of God will be revealed in its fullness.

---

[7] Kenneth R. Samples, "The *Recent* Truth About Seventh-Day Adventism", *Christianity Today*, Vol. 34/2 (5 February 1990), p. 20.
[8] Revelation 14:6-7.

Appendix I: Mission Statement of the Seventh-Day Adventist Church[1]

A 05 05 Our Mission - The Mission of the Seventh-day Adventist Church is to proclaim to all peoples the everlasting gospel in the context of the three angels' messages of Revelation 14:6-12, leading them to accept Jesus as personal Savior and to unite with His church, and nurturing them in preparation for His soon return.

A 05 10 Our Method - We pursue this mission under the guidance of the Holy Spirit through:

1. *Preaching* - Accepting Christ's commission (Matt 28:18-20), we proclaim to all the world the message of a loving God, most fully revealed in His Son's reconciling ministry and atoning death. Recognizing the Bible to be God's infallible revelation of His will, we present its full message, including the second advent of Christ and the continuing authority of His Ten Commandment law with its reminder of the seventh-day Sabbath.

2. *Teaching* - Acknowledging that development of mind and character is essential to God's redemptive plan, we promote the growth of a mature understanding of and relationship to God, His Word, and the created universe.

3. *Healing* - Affirming the biblical emphasis on the well-being of the whole person, we make the preservation of health and the healing of the sick a priority and through our ministry to the poor and oppressed, co-operate with the Creator in His compassionate work of restoration.

A 05 15 Our Vision - In harmony with the great prophecies of the Scriptures, we see as the climax of God's plan the restoration of all His creation to full harmony with His perfect will and righteousness.

---

[1] *General Conference Working Policy* (1998-1999 edition), p. 27.

Appendix II: "The Remnant and Its Mission"[2]

The Universal Church is composed of all who truly believe in Christ, but in the last days, a time of widespread apostasy, a remnant has been called out to keep the commandments of God and the faith of Jesus. This remnant announces the arrival of the judgment hour, proclaims salvation through Christ, and heralds the approach of His second advent. This proclamation is symbolized by the three angels of Revelation 14; it coincides with the work of judgment in heaven and results in a work of repentance and reform on earth. Every believer is called to have a personal part in this worldwide witness.

---

[2] *Seventh-day Adventists Believe*, p. 152.

Annotated Bibliography

Publications by Adventists Referred to

Books

Amundsen, Wesley, *The Advent Message in Inter-America*, RHPA, 1947. [Missionary history.]

Anderson, Harry, *Auf den Pfaden Livingstones*, AV, 1929. [Mission stories]

Bacchiocchi, Samuele, *The Advent Hope for Human Hopelessness: A Theological Study of the Meaning of the Second Advent for Today*, Berrien Springs: by the author, 1986.

Baker, Delbert W., *From Exile to Prime Minister: How Samson Kisekka, a Christian Physician, is Successfully Leading Uganda from Ruin to Restoration*, RHPA, 1988. [A short, somewhat hagiographic work on a prominent SDA politician.]

Bauer, Bruce L., "Congregational and Mission Structures and How the Seventh-Day Adventist Church Has Related to Them", DMiss, Pasadena: Fuller Theological Seminary, 1982.

Baumgartner, Erich W. (ed.), *Re-Visioning Adventist Mission in Europe*, AUP, 1998. [A collection of articles by church leaders and missiologists mainly from the Euro-Africa and Trans-European Divisions. The book focuses on these two divisions, and in these, mainly on its secularized population and Islam, leaving Eastern Europe virtually untouched. Here are found a few excellent articles on the secular person.]

Baumgartner, Erich W. et al. (eds.), *Passport to Mission*, Berrien Springs: Institute of World Mission, 1999. [A concise preparatory course designed mainly for short-term missionaries or volunteers. Touches most important areas of missionary preparation.]

Baumgartner, Erich W., "Towards a Model of Pastoral Leadership for Church Growth in German-Speaking Europe", PhD, Pasadena: Fuller Seminary, 1990.

Beach, Bert Beverly, *... auf daß sie alle eins seien*, ed. by Gemeinschaft der Siebenten-Tags-Adventisten in der DDR [the SDA Church in the (former) GDR], Berlin: Union Verlag, 1977. [The English original which is slightly different is: Bert Beverly Beach, *Ecumenism: Boon or Bane?*, RHPA, 1974. The author is a veteran of SDA inter-denominational relationships. Here he describes the ecumenical movement and the official SDA position on ecumenism.]

Beach, Walter R. and Bert B. Beach, *Role and Function of Church Organization*, RHPA, 1985.

Bruinsma, Reinder, *It's Time to Stop Rehearsing what we Believe and Start Looking at what Difference it Makes*, RHPA, 1998. [An explanation of the existential meaning of the 27 SDA Fundamental Beliefs.]

Christian, Lewis Harrison, *Pioneers and Builders of the Advent Cause in Europe*, PPPA, 1937. [A short mission history that, unfortunately, leaves out L.R. Conradi, a key person in building Adventism in Europe who was Christian's predecessor and who left the SDA Church in the 1930s.]

Damsteegt, P. Gerard, *Foundations of the Seventh-Day Adventist Message and Mission*, Grand Rapids: Eerdmans, 1977. [The development of theological concepts of the Millerite Movement and its aftermath leading to the foundation of the SDA Church.]

Dudley, Roger L., *Plant a Church, Reap a Harvest*, PPPA, 1989. [An SDA call to church planting as central missionary strategy in the Western world.]

Dudley, Roger L., and Des Cummings Jr., *Adventures in Church Growth*, RHPA, 1983. [A well- researched book about SDA growth in North America. Dudley's institute on campus conducts various annual surveys of church growth for the North American Division]

Dunton, Hugh I., Baldur Ed. Pfeiffer, and Borge Schantz (eds.), *Adventist Missions Facing the 21st Century: A Reader*, Archives of International Adventist History 3, Frankfurt: Lang, 1990. [A collection of articles from a 1988 symposium of SDA missiologists held at Newbold College, England. Various unrelated but interesting articles on theology, organization, strategy, and history of missions and women and the family in mission.]

DuPreez, Ronald A.G., "Polygamy in the Bible with Implications for Seventh-Day Adventist Missiology", DMin, AU, 1993. [An attempt to show that polygamy is unacceptable in the Bible. The missiological aspect is discussed rather briefly].

Dybdahl, Jon (ed.), *Adventist Mission in the 21st Century: The Joys and Challenges of Presenting Jesus to a Diverse World*, RHPA, 1999. [A collection of articles by SDA missiologists and leaders on most aspects of SDA missiology: biblical and theological issues, strategies and methods, and case studies. Similar to the content of Hugh I. Dunton et al., *Adventist Missions Facing the 21st Century*, and Erich W. Baumgartner, *Re-Visioning Adventist Mission in Europe*.]

Dybdahl, Jon, *Missions: A Two-Way Street*, PPPA, 1986. [A former missionary in Thailand and leading SDA missiologist reflects on what *he* learnt from the missionary work he was assigned to do.]

Firth, Robert E. (ed.), *Servants for Christ: The Adventist Church Facing the Eighties*, AUP, 1980. [Sections on the World-Wide development of the SDA Church and strategies of church growth.]

Goldstein, Clifford, *The Remnant*, PPPA, 1994.

Handbuch für Gemeindeaufbau, 3 vols., Darmstadt, Friedensau: Zentralstelle für Evangelisation und Gemeindeaufbau, 1993. [A German SDA series of seminars to be held in churches comprising most important aspects of church growth theory.]

Historical Sketches of the Foreign Missions of the Seventh-day Adventists, Basel: Imprimerie Polyglotte, 1886. [The first SDA mission history.]

Howell, Clifford G., *The Advance Guard of Missions*, PPPA, 1912. [About missionary pioneers of other church organizations - many before Adventism, but some also paralleling the SDA history. Interesting that Howell speaks of them all very positively.]

Hole, Jonquil and Borge Schantz (eds.), *The Three Angels and the Crescent: A Reader*, Bracknell: SDA Global Centre for Islamic Studies, 1993. [Papers presented at a 1992 symposium on SDA Mission amongst Muslims, with many very up-to-date articles; sections on regional studies, social issues, theological issues, and evangelism, including an article by evangelical specialist on Muslim evangelism Martin Goldsmith.]

Kisaka, John Aza, "The Adventist Church's Position and Response to Socio-cultural Issues in Africa", DMin, AU, 1979. [A 100 page study of issues such as polygamy, dowry, and ancestor veneration.]

Knight, George R., *A Brief History of Seventh-Day Adventists*, RHPA, 1999. [A concise introductory overview.]

Knight, George R., *Millennial Fever and the End of the World: A Study of Millerite Adventism*, PPPA, 1993. [A detailed 384 page historical study of Millerism.]

Knight, George R., *The Fat Lady and the Kingdom: Adventist Mission Confronts the Challenges of Institutionalism and Secularization*, PPPA, 1995.

Knowles, George E., *How to Help Your Church Grow*, RHPA, 1981; 2nd ed.: Silver Spring: Ministerial Association, General Conference of Seventh-day Adventists, 1997. [An application of Church Growth Theory to the SDA context.]

Kobialka, Martin, *Mehr als Brot: Wesen und Werk der Adventmission*, Frankfurt: by the author, 1975. [Diss. Frankfurt, consisting mainly of statistical materials and historical details from the beginnings of SDA work in many countries of the world.]

Koranteng-Pipim, Samuel, *Receiving the Word: How New Approaches to the Bible impact Our Biblical Faith and Lifestyle*, Berrien Springs: Berean, 1996. [A zealous call for literalist hermeneutics and traditional Adventist interpretation of the Bible.]

Lehmann, Richard, Jack Mahon and Borge Schantz (eds.), *Cast the Net on the Right Side...: Seventh-Day Adventists Face the "Isms" - Crucial Issues for Witnessing to Western People*, Bracknell: European Institute of World Mission, 1993. [SDA Mission amongst the secular and its challenges.]

Lesovsky, Wilhelm, "Islam und Sabbathalter", unpublished Ms, 1936, AEA, N 1-1, 168-200. [Holds that there is a close similarity of proto-Islam and Adventism.]

Mager, Johannes (ed.), *Die Gemeinde und ihr Auftrag*, Studien zur adventistischen Ekklesiologie 2, Hamburg: Saatkorn, 1994. [Articles about the identity of the SDA Church, Adventism and Ecumenism, the church and the world, and other ecclesiological essays.]

Maxwell, Mervyn C., *Tell it to the World: The Story of Seventh-Day Adventists*, PPPA, 1977. [A history that stresses the development of SDA distinctive doctrines.]

Mueller, W., *Der Dienst der Mission*, Hamburg: Vollmer & Bentlin, 1940. [SDA apologetics of mission in the context of Nazi Germany]

Neufeld, Don F. (ed.), *Seventh-Day Adventist Encyclopedia*, RHPA, 1966. [Many historical details of SDA missions can be found here in articles about institutions, countries, missionaries, and converts; however, from a strongly Western point of view; even its CD-ROM version of the late 1990s has only little more material than the original version.]

Noack, Winfried, *Gemeinde mit Zukunft*, AV, n.d. [ca. 1980. Noack draws a picture of a church that is missionary by caring and addressing the needs of people in the contemporary western world.]

Olsen, M. Ellsworth, *A History of the Origin and Progress of Seventh-Day Adventists*, RHPA, 1925. [An early history with many details.]

Oosterwal, Gottfried, *Mission: Possible*, SPA, 1972. [The classical book on SDA missiology by Adventism's first renowned missiologist – a collection of articles calling for mission amongst the secularized, for the unreached and a balanced World-Wide mission programme.]

Oosterwal, Gottfried, *Patterns of Seventh-Day Adventist Church Growth in North America*, AUP, 1976.

Owusu-Mensa, Kofi, *Saturday God and Adventism in Ghana*, Frankfurt: Lang, 1993. [Two books in one: the first half is a study of the Akan High God *Onyamee Kwaame* ("Saturday God"); the second is a brief history of Adventism in Ghana.]

Paulien, Jon, *Present Truth in the Real World: The Adventist Struggle to Keep and Share Faith in a Secular Society*, PPPA, 1993. [An endeavour to show that Adventism needs to address the secular person different from fellow Christians.]

Pfeiffer, Baldur, Lothar E. Träder and George R. Knight (eds.), *Die Adventisten und Hamburg: Von der Ortsgemeinde zur internationalen Bewegung*, Frankfurt: Lang, 1992. [A collection of symposium presentations that show how Adventism grew from one main centre in Germany, Hamburg, to a movement in the whole of Germany and many other countries.]

Pfeiffer, Baldur (ed.), *Seventh-Day Adventist Contributions to East Africa, 1903-1983*, Frankfurt: Lang, 1985. [The editor told me that the idea behind this book was to respond to the charge heard sometimes that Adventism makes converts but does not contribute to society.]

Pfeiffer, Baldur, *The European Adventist Mission in the Middle East, 1879-1939*, Frankfurt: Lang, 1981. [A mission history with fine missiological observations.]

Pöhler, Rolf J., "Change in Seventh-Day Adventist Theology: A Study of the Problem of Doctrinal Development", ThD, AU, 1995. [The first comprehensive study on how Adventist doctrine developed and changed.]

Rasi, Humberto, and Fritz Guy (eds.), *Meeting the Secular Mind: Some Adventist Perspectives*, Selected Working Papers of the Committee on Secularism of the General Conference of SDA 1981-1985, AUP, 1980. [The first SDA book that deals with Adventist witness in the secular world.]

Reid, G. Edward, *Sunday's Coming: Eye-Opening Evidence that These Are the Very Last Days*, by the author, 1996. [An leading North American Adventist's attempt of proving that "Sunday Law" will soon be proclaimed and the end of the world is very near – expected to be in the year 2000.]

Rumi, Abderrahim Al- [pseudonym], *The Qur'an is Right When It Says...*, Ostfildern: Die offene Tür, n.d. [SDA Brochures for Muslims that argue, mostly with the Qur'an, that Muslims should be open for the study of the Bible.]

Sahlin, Monte, *Sharing Your Faith with Your Friends without Losing Either*, RHPA, 1990. [A guide of personal evangelism in a secular world.]

Schantz, Borge F., "The Development of Seventh-Day Adventist Missionary Thought: Contemporary Appraisal", PhD, Pasadena: Fuller Theological Seminary, 1983. [A more than 1000 page dissertation; a large collection of materials concerning the history of general evangelical missiology, the history of SDA missiology, and Ellen White's contribution to it.]

Schantz, Borge F., "Understanding Islam: Introduction to Islam and Muslim Evangelism", Photocopies of Transparencies, [Bracknell:] Global Centre for Islamic Studies, 1991. [Charts about central features of Islam and Evangelism amongst Muslims.]

Schantz, Borge F., *Your Muslim Neighbour and You: A Manual for Personal Evangelism*, Bracknell: SDA Global Centre for Islamic Studies, 1993. [A fine 48 pp. collection of guidelines for sensitive evangelism amongst Muslims.]

Schwarz, R.W., *Light Bearers to the Remnant*, PPPA, 1979. [The college textbook for introductory SDA history courses.]

Seventh-Day Adventists Answer Questions on Doctrine, Washington, D.C.: Ministerial Association, General Conference of Seventh-day Adventists, 1957. [A first official "SDA theology" that was written as a response to a dialogue with evangelicals who inquired the official stand of Adventism on various doctrines.]

Seventh-Day Adventists Believe...: A Biblical Exposition of 27 Fundamental Doctrines, Washington, D.C.: Ministerial Association, General Conference of Seventh-day Adventists, 1988. [A widely circulated book that reflects the most common interpretation of basic SDA beliefs.]

So Much in Common: Documents of Interest in the Conversation Between the World Council of Churches and the Seventh-Day Adventist Church, Geneva: World

Council of Churches, 1973. [A report of a dialogue between representatives of the SDA Church and the WCC.]

Spalding, Arthur Whitefield, *Origin and History of Seventh-Day Adventists*, 4 vols., RHPA, 1961/1962. [An anecdotal approach to SDA history.]

Spicer, William A., *Our Story of Missions*, PPPA, 1921. [Records the beginnings of mission in the fields entered by 1920.]

Staples, Russell L., *Community of Faith: The Seventh-Day Adventist Church in the Contemporary World*, RHPA, 1999. [A theological study of the nature and role of the Church.]

Statements, Guidelines and other Documents - A Compilation, Silver Spring: General Conference Communication Department, 2000. [Since 1980, the SDA Church formulated an increasing number of position statements and guidelines on topics of public interest. They are collected here.]

Watts, Dorothy Eaton, and James Hardin, *Getting Excited about Global Mission*, RHPA, 1989. [A book for Global Mission promoters and fund raisers.]

White, Ellen G., *Christian Service*, RHPA, 1925. [A compilation of Ellen White statements on service.]

White, Ellen G., *Counsels on Stewardship*, RHPA, 1940. [A compilation of Ellen White statements on Christian stewardship.]

White, Ellen G., *Counsels to Parents, Teachers, and Students*, PPPA, 1913.

White, Ellen G., *The Desire of Ages*, RHPA, 1898. [The life of Christ.]

White, Ellen G., *Early Writings*, RHPA, 1892.

White, Ellen G., *Education*, PPPA, 1903.

White, Ellen G., *Evangelism*, RHPA, 1946. [A compilation of Ellen White statements on evangelism.]

White, Ellen G., *Fundamentals of Christian Education*, SPA, 1923. [A compilation of Ellen White statements on Christian education.]

White, Ellen G., *Gospel Workers: Instruction for All who are "Laborers Together with God"*, Rev. and enlarged ed., RHPA, 1948. [1st ed. 1892; 2nd ed. 1915.]

White, Ellen G., *The Great Controversy between Christ and Satan*, PPPA, 1884. [An interpretative presentation of church history until Christ's second coming. The most well-known SDA book.]

White, Ellen G., *Life Sketches of Ellen G. White*, PPPA, 1915.

White, Ellen G., *Manual for Canvassers*, RHPA, 1902. [On literature evangelism.]

White, Ellen G., *The Ministry of Healing*, RHPA, 1905. [Medical and health work as part of the mission of the church; a presentation of "health reform", sometimes called "the right arm of the 3 Angels' messages".]

White, Ellen G., *Selected Messages*, Vol. 1, RHPA, 1958.

White, Ellen G., *The Southern Work*, RHPA, 1966 [Reprinted from articles and letters of 1891-1899].

White, Ellen G., *Testimonies*, 9 vols., PPPA, 1948.

White, Ellen G., *Testimonies to Ministers and Gospel Workers*, PPPA, 1923. [A compilation of Ellen White statements on the pastoral ministry.]
White, Ellen G., *Welfare Ministry*, RHPA, 1952. [A compilation of Ellen White statements on social service.]
White, Ellen G. and James White, *A Word to the "Little Flock"*, Brunswick, Maine: by the authors, 1847; facsimile reproduction, RHPA, n.d.
Wieland, Robert J., *In Search of the Treasure of Faith*, All Africa Publications, n.d., n.p. [An SDA book written for Muslims, presenting biblical doctrine.]
Wieland, Robert J., *The Revelation of Things to Come*, Rev. Ed., All Africa Publications, 1982, n.p. [On the book of Revelation.]
Working Policy of the General Conference of Seventh-Day Adventists: 1995-1996 edition, RHPA, n.d. [Contains guidelines for GC operations.]

Magazines

Adventist Frontiers: News from Adventist Frontier Missions and Missionaries, Berrien Springs, 1985ff. [Reports and promotional material of a growing but independent SDA mission agency.]
Adventist Heritage: A Journal of Adventist History, Loma Linda, 1974ff.
Adventist-Muslim Review, Newbold College, Bracknell, England: SDA Global Centre for Islamic Studies, 1993-1994. [A short-lived but interesting magazine on mission amongst Muslims.]
Adventist-Muslim Relations Net Newsletter, Loma Linda, USA, 1996ff. [The continuation of *Adventist-Muslim Review* under a new editor.]
Adventist News Network. [A weekly email service with official SDA news from the GC Communication Department, Silver Spring.]
Adventist Review, Washington, D.C., and Silver Spring, 1978ff. [The official SDA organ.]
Fides et Libertas: The Journal of the International Religious Liberty Association, Silver Spring, 1998ff.
Gewissen und Freiheit: Offizielles Organ der Internationalen Vereinigung zur Verteidigung und Förderung der Religionsfreiheit, Bern, 1973ff. [French Ed.: Bern; English Ed.: St. Albans; Portuguese Ed.: Lisboa; Spanish Ed.: Madrid]
Journal of Adventist Thought in Africa, Eldoret, 1995ff. [Explores Adventism in relation to various aspects of African history, culture, theology, etc.]
Liberty, RHPA, 1906ff. [Adventist magazine dealing with religious liberty.]
Maranatha: Official Magazine of the 1000 Missionary Movement, Silang (Philippines): 1992ff. [A promotional magazine about this short-term missions movement]
Ministry, Washington, D.C., and Silver Spring, 1928ff. [The SDA magazine for pastors.]
Mission, Washington D.C., 1912ff. [A quarterly with weekly mission report readings for Sabbath School.]

Newsletter of the SDA Global Centre for Islamic Studies, Newbold College, Bracknell, England: 1989-1992. [Predecessor of *Adventist-Muslim Review*]
Philippine Frontiers, Manila 1993ff. [Reports and promotional material of Philippine Frontier Missions, the Filipino equivalent of Adventist Frontier Missions.]
[Second] [Advent] Review and [Sabbath] Herald, 1850-1977. [The official SDA organ, predecessor of *Adventist Review*.]
Spectrum: Journal of the Association of Adventist Forums, Takoma Park, 1968ff. [The magazine of an association of Adventist intellectuals that addresses various critical issues and topics in the field of faith and science.]

Articles and Unpublished Materials

Andrews, John N., "Meeting of Sabbathkeepers in Neuchâtel", RH, Vol. 25 (November 24, 1874), p. 172.
Basaninyenzi, Gatsinzi, "The Gospel and Culture: Lessons from Our Critics", JATA, Vol. 1/1 (Nov. 1995), pp. 110-118.
Baumgartner, Erich, personal conversation with the author, Nairobi, April 1999.
Branson, Roy, "Adventists between the Times: The Shift in the Church's Eschatology", *Spectrum*, Vol. 8/1 (September 1976), pp. 13-26.
"Commissioned to Serve: Adventist Development and Relief Agency", n.d. [Brochure published for the 1995 SDA General Conference session].
"Contextualization and SDA Mission", unpublished Ms, Global Mission Issues Committee, 1998.
"Contextualized Adventist Communities", unpublished Ms, Global Mission Issues Committee, 1999.
Dabrowski, Ray, "New Formula for Financing Adventist Church Mission Voted", ANN (25 April 2000).
Dunton, Hugh I., "Prophets in Parallel: Mohammed and Ellen G. White - Adventism and Islam Share a Respect for the Prophetic Gift", *Spectrum*, Vol. 22/4 (October 1992), pp. 40-51.
Dybdahl, Jon, "Anatomy of the Church Growth Movement", *Spectrum*, Vol. 12/3 (April 1982), pp. 6-10.
Dybdahl, Jon, "Exploring the Challenges", AR, Vol. 172/23 (June 8, 1995 - Special Issue Global Mission), pp. 12f.
Dybdahl, Jon, "Is There Hope for the Unevangelized?", *Dialogue*, Vol. 7/1 (1995), pp. 16-17+29.
Dybdahl, Jon, "The Land That Remains", AR, Vol. 171, (6 October 1994), pp. 40-41+43-44 (1064-1065+1067-1068).
Folkenberg, Robert S., "Church Structure: Servant or Master?" *Ministry*, Vol. 62/6 (June, 1989), pp. 4-9.
Fordham, W.W., "The Remnant Church", *Ministry*, Vol. 43/6 (June 1970), p. 61.

"Fundamental Beliefs and Preparation for Baptism", unpublished Ms, Global Mission Issues Committee, 1999.

Gallagher, Jonathan, "First ever Contextualized Burmese Adventist Church Service", *Adventist News Network*, February 24, 1998.

Getui, Mary, "Women and Mission in the Seventh-Day Adventist (SDA) Church in Kenya", JATA, Vol. 1/1 (November 1995), pp. 75-85.

Gustin, Pat, interview by the author, Nairobi, April 1999.

Höschele, Stefan, "The Islam Conference 1935: Summing up Half a Century of Mission Experience", Term paper, Theologische Hochschule Friedensau, 1993.

"Intentional Outreach", Interview with Michael Ryan, AR, Vol. 172/23 (June 8, 1995), pp. 10-11.

John, Harrison W., "SAWS Expands Its Focus", *Spectrum*, Vol. 12/3 (April 1982), pp. 15-21.

Johnsson, William G., "Between the Ideal and the Actual", AR 163/22 (May 29, 1986), pp. 4-5.

Johnsson, William G., "The Mythos of the Mission Story", *Spectrum*, Vol. 8/1 (September 1976), pp. 40-43.

King, Headley [Pseudonym], "Tentmakers in the Arabian Gulf", *Spectrum*, Vol. 22/4 (October 1992), pp. 33-39.

Knott, Bill, "With All Deliberate Speed: A Study of Pace in Mission", *Spectrum*, Vol. 12/3 (April 1982), pp. 11-14.

Lawson, Ronald, "Broadening the Boundaries of Church-Sect Theory: Insights from the Evolution of the Non-Schismatic Mission Churches of Seventh-Day Adventism", *Journal for the Scientific Study of Religion*, Vol. 37/4 (September 1998), pp. 652-672.

Lawson, Ronald, "Sect-State Relations: Accounting for the Differing Trajectories of Seventh-day Adventists and Jehovah's Witnesses", *Sociology of Religion*, Vol. 56/4 (1995), pp. 351-377.

Maberly, Clifton, personal conversation with the author, Mombasa, December 1997.

Mahon, Jack, "Muslims and Mission: An Introduction", *Spectrum*, Vol. 22/4 (October 1992), pp. 22-24.

N'Getich, Sammy, "Sabbath-Keeping Traditions in Africa: The Case of the Kalenjin People of Kenya", JATA, Vol. 2/1 (November 1996), pp. 45-53.

"131st [One-Hundredth and Thirty-First] Annual Statistical Report - 1993", Silver Spring: General Conference of Seventh-day Adventists, 1994.

Oosterwal, Gottfried, "Adventistische Mission heute", in P. William Dysinger and Yvonne M. Dysinger, "Studienhilfe für Gesundheitsevangelisation", Ms., Adventist International Medical Society, n.d. [early 1990s], pp. 1-18.

Oosterwal, Gottfried, "Converting Entire Peoples", *Spectrum*, Vol. 12/3 (April 1982), pp. 2-5.

Oosterwal, Gottfried, "Gemeindewachstum", Special issue of *Aller Diener*, No. 3-4 (1981), pp. 5-224.

Osindo, Oscar, "Towards a Seventh-Day Adventist Mission to Muslims in Kenya", JATA, Vol. 2/1 (1996), pp. 92-104
"Our Mission and Other Christians", unpublished Ms, Global Mission Working Group, 1996.
Pichot, Marcel, "The Village of Bendougou", *Adventist Frontiers*, Vol. 15/4 (April 1999), p. 21.
Pöhler, Rolf J., "'And the Door was Shut' - Seventh-Day Adventists and the Shut-Door Doctrine in the Decade after the Great Disappointment", unpublished paper, AU, 1978.
Ryan, Michael, "Global Mission and You", *Dialogue* 5/1 (1993), pp. 16-18.
"So Send I You: Biblical Models of Soul-Winning", Adult Sabbath School Lessons, Standard Edition, January-March 1994, Silver Spring: Department of Church Ministries, General Conference of Seventh-day Adventists, 1994.
Staples, Russell, "Adventism", in Donald W. Dayton and Robert K. Johnston (eds.), *The Variety of American Evangelicalism*, Knoxville: Univ. of Tennessee Press, 1991, pp. 57-71.
Staples, Russell, "Contextualization, Church and Confessions", unpublished Ms presented to the Global Mission Issues Committee, 1999. [23 pp.]
Staples, Russell, "The Church and Polygamy in Sub-Saharan Africa: A Working Paper Produced at the Request of the General Conference", unpublished Ms, 1981.
"Stellungnahme der Generalkonferenz hinsichtlich der Beziehungen zu anderen Religionsgemeinschaften", *Aller Diener* (3-4/1984), pp. 59-62.
Taylor, Charles R., "Measuring a Dream", AR, Vol. 172/23 (June 8, 1995), p. 8.
"The Use of Non-Christian Writings in Mission", unpublished Ms, Global Mission Issues Committee, 1998.
"Transitional Organizational Structures", unpublished Ms, Global Mission Issues Committee, 1998.
Twumasi, Sampson K., "The Challenge of Folk Islam in East Africa", JATA, Vol. 3/1 (November 1997), pp. 92-99.
Vierus, Thomas, "Das erkämpfte Bild vom Islam", Thesis, Darmstadt: Theologisches Seminar Marienhöhe, 1991.
Vyhmeister, Nancy, "Women of Mission", *Spectrum*, Vol. 15/4 (December 1984), pp. 38-43.
Whitehouse, Jerald, "Adventist Christians, Cultural Muslims", *Spectrum*, Vol. 22/4 (October 1992), pp. 25-32.
[Whitehouse, Jerald,] "Indicators for each of the Six Steps in Spiritual Growth, to Measure Progress", *Adventist-Muslim Relations Net Newsletter*, Vol. 1 (December 1996), p. 6.
Whitehouse, Jerald, personal conversation with the author, Mombasa, December 1997.

Wiklander, Bertil, "The Boundaries of Contextualisation in Mission: How Flexible and Absolute Are They? What Principles Should Guide the Church?", unpublished Ms presented to the Global Mission Issues Committee, 1998. [25 pp.]
Wolde-Endreas, Solomon, "The Abyssinian Church: History and Missiology, in Hugh I. Dunton et al., *Adventist Missions Facing the 21st Century*, pp. 164-179.
"World Council of Churches/Seventh-Day Adventist Conversation", *Ecumenical Review*, Vol. 24/2 (April 1972), pp. 9-23.
Wyk, Gerhard van, "A Perspective Approach to Contextualization", JATA, Vol. 3/1 (November 1995), pp. 29-44.
Wyk, Gerhard van, "A Practical Theological Perspective on Adventist Theology and Contextualisation", JATA, Vol. 1/1 (November 1995), pp. 132-149.

Non-SDA Materials Referred to

Bosch, David J., *Transforming Mission: Paradigm Shifts in Theology of Mission*, Maryknoll: Orbis, 1991.Coote, Robert T., "Twentieth-Century Shifts in the North American Protestant Missionary Community", *International Bulletin of Missionary Research*, Vol. 22/4 (1998), pp. 152-153.
Fiedler, Klaus, "Shifts in Eschatology - Shifts in Missiology", in Jochen Eber (ed.), *Hope does not Disappoint: Studies in Eschatology. Essays from Different Contexts*, Wheaton: World Evangelical Fellowship, Bangalore: Theological Book Trust, 2001, pp. 163-186.
Fiedler, Klaus, *The Story of Faith Missions*, Oxford: Regnum, 1994.
Gilliland, Dean S., "Context is Critical in 'Islampur' Case", *Evangelical Missions Quarterly*, Vol. 34/4 (October 1998), pp. 415-417.
Johnstone, Patrick, *Operation World*, 5th, rev. ed., Carlisle: OM, 1993.
Parshall, Phil, "Danger! New Directions in Contextualization", *Evangelical Missions Quarterly*, Vol. 34/4 (October 1998), pp. 404-410.
Samples, Kenneth R., "The Recent Truth About Seventh-Day Adventism", *Christianity Today*, Vol. 34/2 (5 February 1990), pp. 18-21.
Stott, John (ed.), *Making Christ Known: Historic Mission Documents from the Lausanne Movement, 1974-1989*, Carlisle: Paternoster, 1996, pp. 1-55.
"The 10/40 Window", Colorado Springs: The AD 2000 & Beyond Movement, n.d.
Travis, John [pseudonym], "Must all Muslims Leave 'Islam' to Follow Jesus?", *Evangelical Missions Quarterly*, Vol. 34/4 (October 1998), pp. 411-415.

Further Reference Materials[1]

General

Bediako, Matthew A., "Global Strategy: Africa", AR (30 July 1987), pp. 8-10.
Burton, Wilbur Arthur, "A History of the Mission of Seventh-Day Adventist Education 1844-1900", PhD, Kansas State University, 1987.
Hirsch, Charles B., "The Global Outlook", AR (4 January 1990), pp. 10-11.
Keough, G. Arthur, "The Global Challenge: Islam", AR (16 July 1987), pp. 9-11.
Moyer, Bruce C., "Seventh-day Adventist Missions Face the Twenty-First Century", STD, San Francisco Theological Seminary, 1987.
Oosterwal, Gottfried, "Is Mission Still Possible?", *Ministry*, Vol. 59/12 (1986), pp. 4-8.
Oosterwal, Gottfried, "Shedding the Gospel's Western Package", AR (October 19, 1989), pp. 9-23.
Oosterwal, Gottfried, "The Mission of the Church", *Ministry*, Vol. 51/2, (1978), pp. 24G-K.
Oosterwal, Gottfried, "The New Shape of Adventist Mission", *Spectrum*, Vol. 7/1 (1975), pp. 44-54.
Provonsha, J.W., "The Church as a Prophetic Minority", *Spectrum*, Vol. 12/1 (1982), pp. 18-23.
Scriven, Charles, "The Real Truth About the Remnant", *Spectrum*, Vol. 17/1 (October 1986), pp. 6-13.
Teel, Charles Jr., "How to Be a Movement, NOT a Machine", *Spectrum*, Vol. 12/1 (1982), pp. 30-33.
Vick, Edward W.H., "Against Isolationism: The Church's Relation to the World", *Spectrum*, Vol. 8/3 (1978), pp. 38-40.

Evangelism and Church Growth

Cerna, Miguel Angel, *The Power of Small Groups in the Church*, Newbury Park: El Camino Publishing, 1991.
Day, Dan, *A Guide to Marketing Adventism*, PPPA, 1990.
Dudley, Roger L., and Des Cummings Jr., "A Study of Factors Relating to Church Growth in the North American Division of Seventh-day Adventists", *Review of Religious Research*, Vol. 24 (1983), pp. 322-333.

---

[1] I thank Erich Baumgartner for sharing his bibliographies on Adventist missions and Church Growth in the SDA context with me. Most of the titles in this section (0) come from these bibliographies. Asterisks (*) refer to non-SDA authors.

Faith Action Advance: Dynamics of Church Growth Manual, ed. by the General Conference of Seventh-day Adventists, RHPA, 1982.

Finley, Mark, *Padded Pews or Open Doors: Seminars that Lead to Decisions*, PPPA, 1988.

*George, Carl, "Challenges Facing Adventists", AR (5 January 1989), pp. 17-20.

*Glasser, Arthur F., "A Friendly Outsider Looks at Seventh-day Adventists", *Ministry*, Vol. 62/1 (January 1989), pp. 8-10.

"Global Strategy of the Seventh-day Adventist Church", AR (11 January 1990), pp. 21-23. [Action voted at the 1989 Annual Council]

Gruesbeck, Clarence, "Applying Church Growth Principles for Effective Ministry in the Seventh-day Adventist Church: Case Study", Doctoral Diss., Pasadena: Fuller Theological Seminary, 1980.

Hubbard, Reuben A., "Master Planning for Church Growth", DMin, Pasadena: Fuller Theological Seminary, 1985.

Sahlin, Monte C., "A Study of Factors Relating to Urban Church Growth in the North American Division of Seventh-day Adventists", Unpublished Report, Berrien Springs: Institute of Church Ministry, Andrews University, 1986.

Sahlin, Monte C., "Global Strategy: North America", AR (6 August 1987), pp. 9-11.

Sahlin, Monte C., *Sharing our Faith with Friends Without Losing Either*, RHPA, 1990.

The Caring Church: A Strategy for North America, ed. by the General Conference of Seventh-day Adventists, North American Division, RHPA, 1983.

*Wagner, C. Peter, "A Church Growth View of Adventists", *Administry* (Winter, 1984), pp. 6-8.

Weeks, Howard B., "A Historical Study of Public Evangelism in the Seventh-Day Adventist Church, 1900-1966", PhD Michigan State University, 1966.

Widmer, Myron, "Global Strategy for Evangelism", AR (2 July 1987), pp. 9-11.

Widmer, Myron, "Enabling the Congregation", AR (5 January 1989), pp. 14-15.

Zackrison, James W., *How to Set Up and Run an Evangelization/Assimilation Cycle in Your Church*, Lincoln: NAD Distribution Center, n.d.

www.ingramcontent.com/pod-product-compliance
Lightning Source LLC
Chambersburg PA
CBHW021813220426
43662CB00006B/297